CONTENTS

Study Guide
to Accompany

WORLD RELIGIONS

Warren Matthews
Old Dominion University

Prepared by

David C. Prejsnar
Community College of Philadelphia

West Publishing Company
St. Paul   New York   Los Angeles   San Francisco

WEST'S COMMITMENT TO THE ENVIRONMENT

In 1906, West Publishing Company began recycling materials left over from the production of books. This began a tradition of efficient and responsible use of resources. Today, up to 95% of our legal books and 70% of our college and school texts are printed on recycled, acid-free stock. West also recycles nearly 22 million pounds of scrap paper annually—the equivalent of 181,717 trees. Since the 1960s, West has devised ways to capture and recycle waste inks, solvents, oils, and vapors created in the printing process. We also recycle plastics of all kinds, wood, glass, corrugated cardboard, and batteries, and have eliminated the use of Styrofoam book packaging. We at West are proud of the longevity and the scope of commitment to the environment.

Production, Prepress, Printing and Binding by West Publishing Company.

TO THE STUDENT

   Your study of world religion is an enterprise that I hope
will at once excite and bewilder, provoke and calm, challenge
and enlighten you. To study the religious experiences of
human beings is to see the cruelty of which people are
capable and to gain hope for the future. Your course in
world religions will teach you about human history, how
different peoples have searched for an Absolute, how they
have tried to explain why bad things happen to them and how
they have expressed these insights in their words, in their
art and in their actions.

   Your textbook, World Religions by Warren Matthews, is
designed to be a readable and exciting introduction to the
field of religious studies. It is written to allow easy
comparisons of the beliefs and practices of the different
religious traditions. This study guide is designed to help
you learn and apply the material you will read in the
textbook. I hope it will be of assistance to you in a number
of ways. The first three parts of each chapter in the guide
are designed to give you an overview of each chapter in the
textbook, and present you with standards to help measure how
well you are mastering the material in the textbook. Part
four challenges you to apply some of the information you have
gained in the textbook to the analysis of primary source
religious documents. The type of analysis you do here should
also assist you in preparing for examinations and paper
assignments. Parts five and six, along with the section on
analyzing texts, should provide you with the tools for
evaluating your understanding of the material in the run-up
to examinations. You will be able to design your own
examination so you can practice taking an exam. Finally,

and, in my own view, most importantly, parts seven, eight and nine of this guide are designed to take you beyond the examination. These sections will help you to work on your critical thinking skills: how to use such skills as analysis, synthesis and comparison to explore the truly exciting problems in the field of religious studies. They will also raise provocative problems for which there are no easy answers. And these sections will challenge you to explore religious experience outside the classroom. Open-ended, critical and committed exploration is the type of learning that will endure long after dates and names have faded from memory.

You have probably already discovered methods of studying that work and help you organize the material and develop your thoughts. If this is the case, use those suggestions I give on how to use this guide that compliment what you already do well. The points that follow are only meant as suggestions. If, on the other hand, you have a difficult time preparing for and doing well on exams, and writing essay papers then you might want to try sticking to the step by step process outlined below. After you have mastered the skills required in the various steps, you can begin to alter them to fit your individual strengths and weaknesses.

Another point to take into consideration when deciding how to use this study guide is how your instructor has structured his course. The type of material your instructor emphasizes and the type of examination he or she will be giving may mean that you will find some parts of this guide more beneficial than others. This book contains a range of practice questions, so use those questions that will best prepare you for your exams.

One final point is to write essays, write research papers, but by all means write. Regardless of the type of examination your instructor will be giving, spend time working on Parts Six through Nine of each chapter. These sections ask you to write essay questions and to examine the implications of what you have studied in the textbook and in class. More than an end in itself, writing helps you synthesize and analyze information. Until you force yourself to write down your ideas, you will be unable to evaluate how much you understand. In addition, writing on these topics will reinforce your memory and aid in the retention of information.

Here are some suggestions on how to use this study guide:

1. Review the Learning Objectives to see which ones you already know. Check off in the book those you think you can accomplish. Keep in mind those you have not mastered.

2. Skim through the vocabulary list. I would suggest comparing the list to the textbook glossary. Check off on the study guide list those items that are in the glossary; these are probably the most important terms. The vocabulary list is meant to be exhaustive. The order of the terms in the list should parallel the order in which they occur in the textbook.

3. Read the chapter in the textbook. I would suggest that you develop a system for highlighting or making notes that works for you. I think that writing notes in the margins is better than highlighting, since it gives you an opportunity to jot down your first ideas and reactions. Through the use of stars or some other symbol, it allows you to grade the importance of each passage. Write down for further inquiry any points you did not understand. Put down any ideas or comments, these might be ideas you will be able to build on when you come to writing an essay.

4. Reread in the book, very quickly, the items you designated as most important.

5. Return to the study guide. Go through the Guided Review, writing down the answer in each blank. The Guided Review parallels the book, so you can easily check your answers. Do this after you complete the review.

6. Pick at least one of the texts in the Analyzing Texts section. Try to apply the material in the textbook to these primary documents. If you have time, write out your analysis. At the end of each chapter in this guide you will find the references for the texts. If you want to do further research on any of these topics, most of the books should be available in a good college library.

7. Give yourself a practice test in order to evaluate your understanding. One of the best ways to prepare for exams is to simulate, as much as possible, the actual examination conditions. Find out what type of questions the instructor usually includes on the exam. Construct a practice examination, using the Self-Test section, one or more essay questions and possibly one of the texts. Try to replicate the examination conditions in terms of time allowed, and access to materials. When you finish the practice exam, check the Answer Key at the end of the chapter. Look up the definitions in the textbook. Critique your essay, looking at how you can improve its writing style and substance.

8. Read through the "Confronting Issues and Answers" section. This section in each chapter examines an issue that has contemporary significance for that particular religious tradition. Consider each issue and how members of that tradition might respond to the issue. You could use this section for brainstorming different ideas, or you could use the issue as the topic for a discussion or a research paper.

9. Read the "Essay for a Deeper Consideration" section. This section is designed to help you improve you writing and analytical skills. Read the "Tips" for each question and try to incorporate them into your essay writing.

10. Finally, try out one or more of the "Projects for Developing Religious Empathy". These projects are designed to be done easily and in a college environment. Each of them is not designed to convert, but rather to expand your awareness of all religions.

Good luck! You will have to work hard to succeed in this course, but you can do it. I hope this study guide allows you to accomplish this task and to make each faith come alive.

ACKNOWLEDGEMENTS .

This study guide reflects my experiences teaching undergraduates about the religions of India, Japan, China, the Near East and the West. I would like to thank all my colleagues who have over the years given me suggestions on teaching and insights into research. Many of their approaches and suggestions have percolated into this guide, in one form or another. I would especially like to thank my colleagues in the History and Philosophy Department at Community College of Philadelphia, and on the Introduction to Humanities course development team, where many of the ideas underlying this guide were debated. A very special note of thanks has to go to Edward Forman, my once and future teaching partner from the English Department. I hope some of his insight into teaching composition has seeped into this volume. Nancy Crochiere at West Publishing deserves my special thanks for her understanding and for answering my one thousand questions.

Finally, for their support, love and laughter during the past six long months, I would like to express my gratitude to my wife, Caroline, and my daughter, Katie.

INTRODUCTION - INTRODUCTION TO RELIGIOUS STUDIES

PART ONE   LEARNING OBJECTIVES

Doing these exercises, in conjunction with reading the textbook, should help you to achieve many of the following objectives. Read them and see how many you already have mastered; then study the following terms and concepts, and work through the exercises. After you have completed all the exercises, review the objectives again.

You should be able to:

1. Explain some of the reasons for the interest in the study of world religions at the university level.

2. Give a definition of "religious studies", and explain how religious studies differs from a "confessional" approach to religion and from theology.

3. Discuss the reasons why scholars undertake the systematic study of religion, and what might be the rewards of such study.

4. Discuss the problem of tension between neutral objectivity and religious involvement as it relates to the academic study of world religions in a secular setting.

5. Know at least six main methodological approaches to the study of religion, and be able to illustrate the characteristics of each approach.

6. Understand the organization of each chapter of the textbook, and the purpose of the different sections of each chapter.

7. Cite and analyze three definitions of "religion" that have been advanced by prominent scholars of religion.

8. Formulate your own definition of "religion", and give some examples of how your definition could be applied to religious beliefs and practices.

PART TWO   TERMS AND INDIVIDUALS

a) Terms and Concepts

religious studies	theology
archaeology	architecture
psychology of religion	anthropology
sociology of religion	history of religions
hieroglyphics	cuneiform
language and literature	myth
philosophy of religion	worldview
Absolute	history
ritual	symbol
religion	ultimate concern
B.C.E.	C.E.

b) Individuals

Walter Houston Clark	Paul Tillich
Rem B. Edwards	Emile Durkheim
Rudolph Otto	Mircea Eliade

PART THREE   GUIDED REVIEW

1. There are many reasons why there is today strong interest in the study of world religions. The author mentions at least three of these sources; explain each source in a sentence:

     a._____.
     b._____.
     c._____.

2. One rationale for including the study of world religions in the curriculum of state institutions is
_____.

3. The study of religion in religiously affiliated institutions often promotes a _____ approach to the study of religion. This differs from the study of religion in secular colleges and universities which _____ this approach.

4. One way of understanding the difference between theology and religious studies is that theology attempts to _____, from the standpoint of _____ _____. On the other hand, religious studies attempts to _____, from the standpoint of _____.

5. Scholars of religious studies, in their role as scholars, try to _____. Yet many religious scholars do , as private individuals, _____.

6. Among the many disciplines that a scholar of religious studies might employ, the academic discipline which excavates and studies the remains of older civilizations is
_____.

7. Religious studies uses the tools and insights of architecture to help analyze, primarily, _____.

8. The anthropologist who emphasized that people should be studied in their own habitat was _____.

9. Art history aids religious studies by studying religious art in order to reveal information about _____.

10. That branch of religious studies that focuses on the origin and development of religious traditions over time is _____.

11. An ancient historian who described the destruction of the Temple in Jerusalem was _____.

12. Scholars of religious studies often have to be able to use many different languages because _____.

13. Among the writing systems that scholars have had to decipher are the picture writing of Egypt called _____, and the wedge-shaped characters of Mesopotamia called _____.

14. The stories that a culture uses to explain things such as how the world began or how the gods affect our lives are called by scholars _____.

15. Philosophy of religion is that branch of philosophy that _____.

16. Psychology of religion studies the role of _____ and _____ in religious experiences and practices.

17. The basic unit of study among sociologists is the _____.

18. The majority of religious traditions have a belief in _____, the highest reality upon which all else depends.

19. The author argues that most religions see a central problem which humans must address, and, in addition, posit a _____ to this problem.

20. The concept of _____ prompts one to refrain from making evaluative judgments about particular religions.

21. Scholars, in trying to understand the beliefs and views of adherents of different religious traditions, need _____, the sharing and appreciation of their emotions and faith.

22. Walter Houston Clark described "religion" as "the inner experience of the individual when he senses a _____".

The best evidence of religion is when the individual "attempts to harmonize his life with the _____".

23. Paul Tillich argued that religion can be understood in terms of a person's _____, and this should be not a particular manifestation but _____.

24. Rem B. Edwards rejected the belief that all religions share some common core. Instead, he argued that religions can best be understood by analyzing their shared _____. Three examples of these might be _____, _____ and _____.

25. Rudolph Otto argued that religion is the feeling of _____ in the presence of the Holy.

PART FOUR   REVIEW OF THE STRUCTURE OF THE TEXTBOOK

Each chapter of the textbook is organized into a number of different sections. Each of these sections is designed to acquaint the student with a different aspect of the religious tradition. After reading the section of the Introduction that explains the organization of each chapter, write in your own words, a short description of the function and nature of each section.

1. Introduction -_____
_____.

2. Historical Development -_____
_____.

3. Worldview -_____
_____.

   a. Absolute_____
_____.

   b. The World_____
_____.

   c. Humans_____
_____.

d. The Problem for Humans_____
_____.

e.The Solution for Humans_____
_____.

f. Community and Ethics_____
_____.

g. An Interpretation of History_____
_____.

h. Rituals and Symbols_____
_____.

i. Life After Death _____
_____.

j. Relationship to Other Religions_____
_____.

4. Current Problems and Issues_____
_____.

5. A Deeper Consideration_____
_____.

6. Resources for Study_____
_____.

PART FIVE   ANALYZING TEXTS

Below are two texts that were not in the textbook. Both
texts, however, do contain ideas and concepts with which you
should be familiar after reading the textbook. Read each
text carefully, and try to analyze each by answering the
following questions: What are the main ideas in the text?
What viewpoint or viewpoints might the author of the text
represent? Is it possible to identify the specific thinker,
discipline, movement, tradition or work from which the text
derives? What intellectual, literary, social, cultural or
historical influences are reflected in the text? For each of

your conclusions, try to point to specific evidence in the text (e.g. terms, ideas, arguments, writing style, etc.) which supports your conclusion. Be careful that your conclusions do not exceed the evidence upon which they rest.

TEXT ONE

Culture consists of the totality of man's products. Some of these are material, others are not. Man produces tools of every conceivable kind, by means of which he modifies his physical environment and bends nature to his will. Man also produces language, and on its foundation and by means of it, a towering edifice of symbols that permeate every aspect of his life. .... Society is constituted and maintained by acting human beings. It has no reality, apart from this activity. Its patterns, always relative in time and space, are not given in nature, nor can they be deduced in any specific manner from the "nature of man". What appears at any particular historical moment as "human nature" is itself a product of man's world-building activity. . . . The "stuff" out of which society and all its formations are made is human meanings externalized in human activity. . . . . It may now be understandable if the proposition is made that the socially constructed world is, above all, an ordering of experience. A meaningful order, or nomos, is imposed upon the discrete experiences and meanings of individuals. To say that society is a world-building enterprise is to say that it is ordering, or nomizing, activity. . . . . Religion is the human enterprise by which a sacred cosmos is established. Put differently, religion is cosmization in a sacred mode. By sacred is meant here a quality of mysterious and awesome power, other than man and yet related to him, which is believed to reside in certain objects of experience.. . . . Every society is engaged in the never completed enterprise of building a humanly meaningful world. Cosmization implies the identification of this humanly meaningful world with the world as such, the former now being grounded in the latter, reflecting it or being derived from it in its fundamental structures. . . . . It can thus be said that religion has played a strategic part in the human enterprise of world-building. Religion implies the farthest reach of man's self-externalization, of his infusion of reality with his own meanings. Religion implies that human order is projected into the totality of being. Put differently, religion is the audacious attempt to conceive of the entire universe as being humanly significant. [1]

TEXT TWO

Meanwhile the very fact that [proposed definitions of "religion"] are so many and so different from one another is enough to prove that the word "religion" cannot stand for any single principle or essence, but rather is a collective name. The theorizing mind tends always to the oversimplification of its materials. . . . . Let us not fall immediately into a one-sided view of our subject, but let us rather admit freely at the outset that we may very likely find no one essence, but many characters which may alternately be equally important to religion. . . . At the outset we are struck by one great partition which divides the religious field. On the one side of it lies institutional, on the other personal religion. As M. P. Sabatier says, one branch of religion keeps the divinity, another keeps man most in view. . . . Now in these lectures I propose to ignore the institutional branch entirely, to say nothing of the ecclesiastical organization, to consider as little as possible the systematic theology and the ideas about the gods themselves, and to confine myself as far as I can to personal religion pure and simple. . . . . Religion, therefore, as I now ask you arbitrarily to take it, shall mean for us the feelings, acts, and experiences of individual men in their solitude, so far as they apprehend themselves to stand in relation to whatever they may consider the divine. [2]

PART SIX   SELF-TEST

A) Definitions and Descriptions - Write your own definition or description of each of the following terms. After completing the self-test, check your answer with the definition or description given in the textbook.

1.History of Religions _____
_____
_____.

2.Myth_____
_____
_____.

3.B.C.E._____
_____
_____.

4.Religious studies_____
_____
_____.

5.Psychology of Religion_____
_____
_____.

6.Theology_____
_____
_____.

7.Philosopy of religion_____
_____
_____.

8.Ritual_____
_____
_____.

B)Multiple choice

1. Which of the following structures is probably not of
   interest to religious studies scholars using the tools of
   architecture?

   a. Schools
   b. Pagodas
   c. Churchs
   d. Pyramids

2. Paul Tillich's definition of religion revolved around what central idea?

   a. Belief in a "Beyond".
   b. The feeling of awe in the presence of the Holy.
   c. The use of symbols and rites.
   d. Ultimate concern about something.

3. The discipline that attempts to explain and justify the doctrines of a particular religious tradition from the standpoint of a member of that tradition is called

   a. Theosophy
   b. Religious studies
   c. Theology
   d. Anthoropology

4. The author lists a number of sources for increased interest in world religions. Which of the following is not mentioned as a source?

   a. Increased ease and amount of world travel.
   b. Increased numbers of international missionaries.
   c. The growth towards a "one world" financial market.
   d. Increased numbers of students studying abroad.

5. The historian who described the Roman destruction of the Temple in Jerusalem in 70 C.E. was

   a. Herodotus
   b. Philo
   c. Josephus
   d. Cicero

6. The sociologist who argued that gods are little more than society in disguise was

   a. Emile Durkheim
   b. Rudoph Otto
   c. Peter Berger
   d. Mircea Eliade

7. The wedge-shaped characters used in the ancient writings
of Mesopotamia are called

   a. Hieroglyphics
   b. Cuneiform
   c. Letters
   d. Kanji

8. Which of the following seems to best describe the
interests of philosophers of religion?

   a. They study the myths and legends of a religion.
   b. They attempt to examine religious beliefs in order to
      disprove them.
   c. They attempt to examine the rational justification
      of religious beliefs.
   d. They study the role of the emotions and feelings in
      religion.

9. Which of the following is true about religious studies?

   a. Only committed believers can be scholars of religious
      studies.
   b. Scholars of religious studies try to understand the
      views of various traditions without judging their
      truth or falsity.
   c. Scholars of religious studies can not participate in
      any religion.
   d. Almost all scholars of religion adopt a "confessional"
      approach.

10. Sociology of religion is that branch of sociology
that studies

   a. Religious beliefs.
   b. Religious leaders.
   c. Religious experiences.
   d. Religious groups.

C) True-False

T   F   1. Walter Houston Clark's definition of religion
          seems to apply better to the Asian religions than to
          the religions of the Near East.

T   F   2. While perhaps originally not having religious studies among their curricula, many state institutions have recently added courses in this area.

T F   3. That discipline which seeks to uncover and examine the material remains and ruins of cultures of the past is called archaeology.

T F   4. The textbook argues that most religions have a belief in a personal Absolute.

T F   5. In order to maintain their objectivity, it is very important that religious scholars do not believe in any of the world religions.

T F   6. Psychologists of religion may be interested in analyzing states of religious experience such as those found in meditation or prayer.

T F   7. Rather than searching for a core characteristic that all religious traditions share, Rem B. Edwards believes it is more helpful to think of religions in terms of "family traits".

T F   8. Myths and folk tales will be important for the study of some nonliterate people, but will not be for the study of literate people.

T F   9. The anthropologist who at the beginning of the twentieth century inspired others to live among the people they examined and study them in their habitats was Franz Boas.

T F   10. The author of the textbook attempts not to judge whether any particular religion is true or false.

PART SEVEN   ESSAY AND DISCUSSION QUESTIONS

1. Discuss why you are interested in the study of world religions. Are you interested for any of the reasons mentioned in the textbook?

2. The text explains that while religious studies is a separate discipline at many universities and colleges, a religious scholar often uses the methods and techniques of other disciplines. Choose three of the academic disciplines mentioned in the Introduction to the textbook. Construct a conversation between three scholars each of whom belong to one of these disciplines. In this conversation have each scholar explain to the others what is the approach of his discipline, and how this approach might be useful to a person attempting to understand world religions. Towards the end of the conversation have the scholars discuss the question of whether using a variety of their approaches would be best for understanding world religions.

3. Why might people who engage in religious studies feel a tension between, on the one hand, maintaining their objectivity and, on the other hand, having empathy for the feelings of religious believers? What are some of the ways one might deal with this tension? How do you see yourself addressing this issue as you study world religion this semester?

4. Compare and contrast the meanings of the term "religion" given by Clark, Tillich and Edwards. What do you think are the strengths and weaknesses of each definition? Why?

PART EIGHT   AN ESSAY FOR DEEPER CONSIDERATION

Essay question

   At the end of this term you will know much more about religion than you do now. However, it might be interesting for you to think and write about how you view "religion" at the start of your study. You might then want to see if your view of "religion" has changed significantly when you have completed this course.   Therefore, write an essay in which you formulate a general definition of "religion". After stating your definition, explain why you believe this to be the most useful definition for understanding different world religions.

<u>Tips for answering</u>:

First, note that you are <u>not</u> being asked to state what you think is the best religion, or the truest religion. Rather, you are being asked to try to come up with a definition of religion that you think will apply to all movements, beliefs or practices that you would consider "religious". You should ask yourself, therefore, whether your definition is too narrow, and applies to only certain types of religions, or certain aspects of religion. But be careful that your definition does not become so broad that it would apply to movements or practices that you would not consider to be "religious" (for example, the Boy Scouts or political parties).

It might be helpful to bear in mind a distinction that many philosophers make when dealing with definitions. Some definitions are what could be termed "definition reports"; that is to say, they attempt to report on how this word or term is actually used by groups of people who speak the language. Dictionaries are the most obvious place to find definition reports. Other definitions, however, are "definition proposals"; an individual proposes to use a word or term in a unique manner in order, perhaps, to isolate the essence of what a word means. The definitions advanced by Clark, Tillich and Edwards in the textbook seem to fall into the category of "definition proposals". In your essay you can make use of both of these types of definitions. For example, you might want to quote and examine dictionary definitions. Notice, however, that the question is asking you to give <u>your</u> own definition proposal, so you probably will only want to use dictionary definitions as a starting point. A proposal need take notice of, but not be limited by, actual usage. Similarly, in your essay you might want to refer to and critique the different proposals mentioned in the text. Just remember that your goal is to formulate your own definition. Such a definition may improve on one of the definitions given in the text, or it might try to combine two of the proposals so as to strengthen the definition.

Finally, the essay question asks that you explain why you believe this definition would be helpful in understanding what is religion. There are a number of ways in which you could approach this task. Notice, for example, how the textbook critiques the proposals by Clark and Tillich; it tries to apply these definitions to actual religious

traditions such as Judaism and Buddhism. At this point in
your study you might not be familiar with a wide variety of
religious traditions. Still, most people do have knowledge
of a few different traditions. In your essay you might try
to apply your definition to a couple of the religions with
which you might be familiar at this time. Do these religious
traditions fit with your definition?

PART NINE   PROJECTS FOR DEVELOPING RELIGIOUS EMPATHY

1. Many of us have friends or acquaintances who are adherents
   of different religious traditions, or who were raised in
   families that believed in other religions. Get together
   a couple of classmates or friends with backgrounds in
   religions other than our own. You might want to ask people
   from this class, or explain to your friends outside class
   this is a project for a class. Ask everyone to talk about
   what religion means to them. What religious tradition did
   they grow up with, or do they believe in now? What role
   does religion play in their lives? Do they identify with
   being a member of a religious group, or do they see
   religion as more of an individual matter? Ask everyone in
   the group to try and not judge or evaluate the beliefs of
   the other people, but to understand and appreciate their
   beliefs.

   Notice whether you and the other members of the group can
   be empathic without judging or trying to convert. What
   sorts of problems might there be in trying to talk about
   religion in this way? How might this be relevant to the
   study of different religions in this class?

2. Increasingly, our society is becoming a multi-religious
   society. Not only are there libel to be Roman
   Catholic and different Protestant denominations in most
   communities, but often many communities have groups of
   Jewish, Islamic, Hindu, Buddhist or other religious
   adherents.

   Get together with a classmate or friend, and by using the
   Yellow Pages of the telephone directory try and locate a
   variety of religious group in your town or city. Write
   down where they have their church, synagogue, temple or
   mosque. Then take a trip or walk to observe the buildings
   that house the different religious communities. Where is

the building located - in the city, in the country, on a
hill? What is the size of the building? What is the
shape of the building? How does it use space? Are there
any unusual elements or shapes in the building? If so,
what might be the reason for including them? Out of what
is the building constructed? What appears to be the
function or purpose of the building? Do the answers to
any of these questions tell you anything about the nature
of the religious community or their beliefs or practices?
How do the different buildings vary? Are the variations
significant, do you think?

3. Go to your college library and try to locate on the
   shelves a recent textbook for Sociology, Art History,
   Anthropology and Philosophy. Skim each book to find
   sections that deal with religion. How does each one deal
   with religion? What approach does each text seem to take
   in its study of religion? How do the textbooks differ in
   how they discuss religion? Do any not deal with religion
   at all? Which approach or approaches seem to be most
   similar to the approach that this class seems likely to
   adopt? Which ones seem most interesting to you? Why?

ANSWER KEY TO SELF-TEST SECTION

b) <u>Multiple choice</u>

1. a   6. a
2. d   7. b
3. c   8. c
4. b   9. b
5. c   10. d

c) <u>True-False</u>

1. F   6. T
2. T   7. T
3. T   8. F
4. F   9. T
5. F   10. T

Notes

[1] Peter L. Berger, <u>The Sacred Canopy: Elements of a Sociological Theory of Religion</u> (Garden City, New York: Anchor Books, 1969) 6-7, 8, 19, 25, 27-28.
[2] William James, <u>The Varieties of Religious Experience: A Study in Human Nature</u> (New York: Modern Library, 1902) 29-32.

Chapter 1

RELIGIONS OF
NONLITERATE PEOPLES

PART ONE   LEARNING OBJECTIVES

Doing these exercises, in conjunction with reading the
textbook, should help you to achieve the following
objectives. Read them and see how many you already have
mastered; then study the following terms and concepts, and
work through the exercises. After you have completed all the
exercises, return to this section and review the objectives
again.

You should be able to:

1. Explain the differences and similarities between the
religions of nonliterate people and the major world
religions.

2. Discuss the religion of a hunting people, the Naskapi, and
demonstrate your knowledge of this religion by using specific

examples of their beliefs and practices. In particular, you should be able to delineate the Naskapi beliefs concerning the soul, the hunt and dreams.

3. Analyze what roles dreams can play in religion, and illustrate that you know Freud's and Jung's basic theories of dream interpretation.

4. Discuss the religion of an agricultural people, the Powhatan people, and demonstrate your knowledge of this religion by using specific examples of their beliefs and practices. In particular, you should be able to talk and write on the Powhatan views and practices concerning medicine and religion, the gods, and divination and magic.

5. Discuss the religion of a second agricultural people, the Cherokee peoples, and demonstrate your knowledge of this religion by using specific examples of their beliefs and practices. In particular, you should be able to talk and write specifically on the Cherokee worldview stories.

6. Differentiate between various definitions of the concept of "worldview stories" or "myths", illustrate the theories of at least three scholars on the role of myth in religion, and analyze these various views on myth.

7. Discuss the religion of the Basongye of Zaire, and demonstrate your knowledge of this religion by referring to specific examples of their beliefs and practices. In particular, you should be able to talk and write convincingly on the Basongye belief in and use of magic.

8. Explain at least three different theories of the definition and role of magic, and demonstrate how these theories could apply to the beliefs of nonliterate peoples.

9. List some of the general features of the religions of nonliterate peoples, and give examples from the religions studied that illustrate these features.

PART TWO   TERMS AND INDIVIDUALS

A) Terms and Concepts

the Naskapi people   mantu
shaman   Mista'peo
Tsaka'bec   trickster
Caribou Man   reincarnation
archetypes   Powhatan Peoples
mamanatowick   weroances
wisakon   weroansquas
Okeus   Ahone
huskanaw   Cherokees
myth   worldview
eternal return   Basongye people
Efile Mukulu   Kafilefile
buchi   kikudu
mankishi   mikishi
magic   corn woman

D) Individuals and Terms from Other Traditions
C. G. Jung   Joseph (Genesis-Exodus)
Joseph (New Testament)   Hippocrates
Plato   Asklepius
Sigmund Freud   Artemidorus
Joseph Campbell

PART THREE   GUIDED REVIEW

1. The largest difference between the religions of
nonliterate people and the major world religions is that in
the religions of nonliterate people there are no

_____.

2. Scholars disagree over the degree to which the religious
practices, beliefs and artifacts of contemporary nonliterate
people can be used to _____.

3. The religious practices and stories of nonliterate people
often deal with the struggle for _____.

4. The textbook classifies the religion of the Naskapi people
as a religion of _____.

5. The Naskapi may not have converted to Christianity because they believe that their ancient religion, unlike Christianity, can help them _____.

6. The Naskapi believe that stars, fish, trees and humans are all filled with _____ or, in their language, _____.

7. A shaman is defined as _____.

8. The essential person, who is located in the heart and is the active soul of each person, is called the _____.

9. The figure in myths who is able to use his wits and cleverness to achieve his ends is called by scholars a _____.

10. While the Naskapi believe that using the proper hunting tools and having hunting skills are relevant to a successful hunt, even more important is _____. This often occurs in _____.

11. The belief that dreams can be used to reveal the truth is not limited to the cultures of nonliterate people; among other cultures that believed dreams could be used to reveal the truth were the _____ and the _____.

12. The figures and themes that Jung believed were common to the dreams of all people are called _____.

13. A major difference between the Naskapi and the Powhaten peoples is that the Powhaten _____.

14. The great king who ruled the Powhaten people was called a _____, and he ruled his area through the _____, who were _____.

15. According to the Powhaten, two activities that were grouped together were _____ and _____.

16. The Powhaten believed in a good god, _____. Even more attention was given to the deity of ill-will, _____. The reason for giving more attention to the latter may be because the Powhaten wanted to

_____.

17. The English believed that during the huskanaw ceremony what occurred was _____. However, modern scholars now believe that what occurred was actually _____.

18. Much of the religion of the Cherokees revolved around _____, which were open only to _____.

19. The Cherokees explain the creation of the earth in the following manner: _____
_____.

20. Animals such as the panther and the owl can see at night because _____.

21. The Cherokees believe that today they have to hunt for game because at one time _____.

22. The story of the "corn woman" is shared by the Cherokees and other native American peoples; it is the story of a woman who can _____.

23. Ake Hultkrantz defines a "worldview" as _____
_____.

24. Nonliterate peoples often see their existence as being cyclical, involving an annual renewal of the earth and themselves. This effort to renew the creation itself is termed by scholars the theme of _____.

25. Lauri Honko gives four criteria to consider when looking at "myths": a) _____
b) _____,
c) _____, and
d) _____.

26. _____ argues that myths are concerned with the beginnings of things, and in so doing serves as a model for human behavior in the present.

27. Alan P. Merriam did a study in the twentieth century of the _____ of who live in _____.

28. The people Merriam studied believe in a good deity, _____, and in an evil deity, _____.

29. While the Basongye people believe in gods, their religion is much more concerned, for example, with _____ and _____.

30. For the people of the village of Lupupa Ngye, the most essential part of a human is his _____.

31. If a Lupupan couple wanted to have a child, they might very well employ a _____.

32. Every aspect of the daily lives of the Basongye people is influenced by _____. Among the people one might find engaging in this practice are _____ and _____.

33. _____ believed that magic was a lower stage in man's development than religion. He also argued that the practitioner of magic believed that his rituals could _____ the world and the gods.

34. Marcel Mauss argued that while magic and religion are practiced in the same society, religion can be characterized as _____, while magic is _____.

35. The author of the textbook claims that nonliterate people often focus their attention on gods or forces that _____.

36. The best way to characterize the relationship between humans and animals in many nonliterate societies is that they _____.

37. In seeking to overcome their problems, nonliterate people often seek to gain control over _____.

38. In the villages of many nonliterate peoples some of the space is defined as _____, while other space is seen as _____.

39. Despite their differences, the beliefs and practices of literate peoples often _____ those of nonliterate peoples.

PART FOUR   ANALYZING TEXTS

In each subsequent chapter of this study guide you will be
asked to read and analyze scriptures taken from the religious
traditions discussed in that particular chapter. These texts
will contain ideas and concepts with which you should be
familiar after reading the textbook. In the case of this
chapter, "The Religions of Nonliterate People", this is, of
course, impossible. The tribes or people studied in this
chapter did not write down their beliefs or stories.
However, the textbook does describe the beliefs and practices
of a number of these peoples. Running through these
descriptions are a number of shared characteristics;
characteristics that the textbook helps to isolate.

Below are three passages written by famous scholars of
religion. Each passage deals with one aspects of religious
expression, an aspect which is important in the religious
expressions of nonliterate peoples. Read each passage
carefully, and try to analyze it by addressing the following
questions: Upon what aspect of religion does the passage
focus? What examples of this function or idea can you find
in the religions discussed in the textbook? Do the examples
provided in the textbook support the position taken in the
passage, or do they support a different position? Does the
textbook provide examples of scholars of religion who have
taken different views of this subject?

TEXT ONE

    Let us consider the deepest and most fundamental element
    in all strong and sincerely felt religious emotion. . .
    If we do so we shall find we are dealing with something
    for which there is only one appropriate expression,
    "mysterium tremendum". The feeling of it may at times
    come sweeping like a gentle tide, pervading the mind
    with a tranquil mood of deepest worship. It may pass
    over into a more set and lasting attitude of the soul,
    continuing, as it were, thrillingly vibrant and
    resonant, until at last it dies away and the soul
    resumes its "profane," non-religious mood of everyday
    experience. It may burst in sudden eruption up from the
    depths of the soul with spasms and convulsions, or lead
    to the strangest excitements, to intoxicated frenzy, to

transport, and to ecstasy. . . . Conceptually <u>mysterium</u>
denotes merely that which is hidden and esoteric, that
which is beyond conception of understanding,
extraordinary and unfamiliar. . . . <u>Tremor</u> is in itself
merely the perfectly familiar and "natural" emotion of
<u>fear</u>. But here the term is taken, aptly enough but
still only by analogy, to denote a quite specific kind
of emotional response, wholly distinct from that of
being afraid, though it so far resembles it that the
analogy of fear may be used to throw light upon its
nature. . . To "keep a thing holy in the heart" means to
mark it off by a feeling of peculiar dread, not to be
mistaken for any ordinary dread . . . [1]

TEXT TWO

It is now possible to approach the main distinction
between myths and folktales, a source of unbounded
confusion in nearly all discussion of myths. Is it
really feasible to separate the two? . . . I would offer
a preliminary and incomplete definition of folktales,
independently of their association with any type of
society or level of culture, as follows: they are
traditional tales, of no firmly established form, in
which supernatural elements are subsidiary; they are
not primarily concerned with 'serious' subjects or the
reflexion of deep problems and preoccupations; and
their first appeal lies in their narrative interest. . .
What are usually termed 'myths" . . . tend to behave
differently. The characters, particularly the hero, are
specific, and their family relationships are carefully
noted . . . The action is complicated, and often broken
up into loosely related episodes. It does not usually
depend on disguises and tricks, but rather on the
unpredictable reactions of individuals, personalities
rather than types. Indeed one of the distinguishing
characteristics of myths is their free-ranging and often
paradoxical fantasy. . . In addition, myths tend to
possess that element of 'seriousness', in establishing
and confirming rights and institutions or exploring and
reflecting problems or preoccupations . . . For myths,
specific though they may be in their characters and
local settings, are usually envisaged as taking place in
a timeless past. . . The action of folktales, on the
other hand, is assumed to have taken place within

historical time, in the past often enough, but not the distant or primeval past.[2]

TEXT THREE

The most elementary forms of behavior motivated by religious or magical factors are oriented to this world. Even human sacrifices, uncommon among urban peoples, were performed in the Phoenician maritime cities without any otherworldly expectations whatsoever. Furthermore, religiously or magically motivated behavior is relatively rational behavior, especially in its earliest manifestations. It follows rules of experience, though it is not necessarily action in accordance with a means-end schema. Rubbing will elicit sparks from pieces of wood, and in like fashion the simulative actions of a magician will evoke rain from the heavens. . . . . Thus, religious or magical behavior or thinking must not be set apart from the range of everyday purposive conduct, particularly since even the ends of the religious and magical actions are predominantly economic. [3]

PART FIVE   SELF-TEST

A) Definitions and Descriptions - Write your own definition or description of each of the following terms. After completing the self-test, check your answer with the definition or description given in the textbook.

1. Okeus _____
_____
_____.

2. huskanaw _____
_____
_____.

3. magic (Marcel Mauss)_____
_____
_____.

4. Efile Mukulu _____
_____
_____.

5. worldview (Ake Hultkrantz) _____
_____
_____.

6. weroances _____
_____
_____.

7. Mista'peo _____
_____
_____.

8. shaman_____
_____
_____.

9. mikishi _____
_____
_____.

   10. trickster_____
_____
_____.

B) Multiple choice

1. Which of the following peoples is mentioned in this
chapter as a nonliterate, hunting people?

    a. Cherokees
    b. Naskapi
    c. Hebrews
    d. Powhatan

2. If a Lupapan couple wanted to make sure they had a child
   probably would

    a. Use a small carved figure.
    b. Consult with a shaman over the meaning of their dreams.
    c. Pray to Efile Mukulu.
    d. Pray to Kafilefil.

3. Which of the following would it be <u>incorrect</u> to say about Tsaka'bec?

    a. He is the man in the moon.
    b. He is a trickster.
    c. He is the Caribou Man.
    d. He is a central figure in the Naskapi myths.

4. Which of the following is <u>not</u> one of Lauri Honko's criteria for understanding <u>myths</u>?

    a. Form
    b. Function
    c. Context
    d. Intent

5. Which of the following historical figures is <u>not</u> mentioned as having studied the significance of dreams?

    a. C. G. Jung
    b. Hippocrates
    c. Sigmund Freud
    d. Aristotle

6. According to the Naskapi people the world is filled with

    a. mamanatowick
    b. mista'peo
    c. mantu
    d. myth

7. The scholar who argued that magic was a more primitive stage in human development than religion was

    a. James G. Frazer
    b. Marcel Mauss
    c. Maxwell Gay Marwick
    d. Donald R. Hall

8. The greatest difference between the religions of peoples in this chapter, and major world religions is that

    a. Major world religions do not make use of myths.
    b. Major world religions write about their beliefs.
    c. The religions in this chapter use dream interpretation.

    d. The religions in this chapter were developed in
       city-states.

9. The Powhatan people classified religion together with

    a. witchcraft
    b. agriculture
    c. law
    d. medicine

10. Which of the following stories is not mentioned as one of
the Cherokee myths?

    a. The story of how the flood covered the earth.
    b. The story of how the earth was created.
    c. The story of how the first human was born.
    d. The story of why Indians must hunt.

C) True-False

T F   1. Many scholars today reject the theories
           concerning magic of both Frazier and Maus.

T F   2. An archetype can be defined as the
           appearance in dreams of the material of the
           Id repressed by the Superego.

T F   3. The Cherokees had a myth about the corn
           woman, who produced corn by rubbing
           her stomach.

T F   4. A major problem for anthropologists dealing
           with contemporary nonliterate peoples is
           determining how much they have been
           influenced by literate peoples.

T F   5. The Powhatan Indians kept the bodies of
           their dead commanders in loaf-shaped
           temples.

T F   6. Scholars have generally agreed on how to
           interpret clues relating to the religious
           practices of ancient nonliterate peoples.

T F   7. The Basongye religion believes that the
                 person is composed of his body and his
                 shadow, but do not have any notion of a
                 spirit or soul.

T F   8. The most important myth for the Naskapi
                 people is their creation myth.

T F   9. The Naskapis believe that communication with
                 the souls of animals is more important than
                 the skill of the hunter.

T F   10. For many nonliterate people the role of the
                 good gods may not be as important as that of
                 malevolent deities or spirits.

PART SIX   ESSAY AND DISCUSSION QUESTIONS

1. Describe what you believe are the most important qualities
   and characteristics that distinguish religions of
   nonliterate people from those of more advanced
   civilizations? What do these characteristics tell us
   about the nature of religion among nonliterate people?

2. Compare and contrast the religion of a hunting people to
   the religion of an agricultural people, choosing one
   agricultural and one hunting culture from those you have
   studied in the textbook. What are the differences and the
   similarities in the beliefs, myths, and rituals of the two
   peoples?

3. "Power" plays an important role in many of the religions
   described in this chapter; power over the hunt, over
   other people, over shamans or witches. How might you
   define "power" in the context of nonliterate cultures?
   What role does "power" play in the religions of
   nonliterate cultures? Why might cultures such as those
   discussed here be concerned with power?

4. What role does magic play in the religions of nonliterate
   peoples? How would you define "magic", and what is its
   relation to religion?

5. Explain Freud's and Jung's theories concerning dreams.
   Do the theories of either man help us to understand dreams
   and their role in the religions of nonliterate people?

PART SEVEN   CONFRONTING QUESTIONS AND ISSUES

     The textbook does not have a "Questions and Issues"
section in this chapter. However, as the textbook states,
many of the elements found in the religions of nonliterate
peoples are also present in the major world religions.
Almost all religious traditions have included within
themselves myths, the use of magical practices and the
interpretation of dreams. And yet, how relevant are such
elements for religion in the modern age? Given advances in
the fields of history, science and psychology, can, and
should, religions continue to employ myths, magic and dreams?
Are such elements an important and necessary part of
religious experience? Or are they the outdated heritage of
the nonliterate, non-rational religions of the past?

     By considering the following problem you might uncover
your views on religion for modern man. Choose a religious
tradition with which you are familiar. It may be, if you
wish, a tradition in which you actually believe and
participate. Or it may be one which you have studied,
perhaps one of the traditions you read about in this chapter.
Imagine, in either case, that you are an active participant
in this tradition. One night you have a dream which could be
interpreted as having religious significance. Perhaps a
famous religious figure from history appears in the dream,
giving you a message. Or maybe the dream contains a message
on how to live you life according to the values of this
tradition. Just make sure you select a dream that would be
relevant for the tradition you have chosen. How would you
choose to deal with this dream? Would you see it as having
religious or spiritual significance and make changes in your
life because of the dream? Or would you interpret the dream
in a non-religious manner? In either case, why would you
choose this approach to the dream? What does your position
concerning the significance of the dream tell you about your
view of religion's role in the modern age? Is it possible
for you, living in the Twentieth Century, to view dreams, in
the manner of the Naskapi, as religious messages?

PART EIGHT   AN ESSAY FOR DEEPER CONSIDERATION

Essay Question

Describe, in your own words, one of the myths of a
nonliterate society discussed in this chapter, as well as,
the function it performs in the society.

Tips For Answering

In subsequent chapters of this study guide you will be
asked to write on more complex essay questions. This
question asks you to develop your essay along somewhat
simpler lines, but is still complex enough to challenge ones
writing and analytical skills, and to benefit from a brief
analysis.

This essay question is basically asking you to give a
description, or, actually, two descriptions. A description
of something might be defined as giving in words an account
of the nature, or appearance, or key points, or function of
that thing. First, the question is asking you to describe a
myth from a nonliterate religious tradition. Second, it is
asking you to describe the myth's function in the society.
The first type of description is the simpler of the two.

You are being asked to choose and describe one of the
myths you have studied. This description will be essentially
a retelling of that myth. In all but very unusual cases your
description of this myth will not be based on work in the
field, but on the description of the myth given in the
textbook. What you will be doing, therefore, is paraphrasing
the description given in the textbook. While rhetoricians
differ in their exact definitions of "paraphrasing", the
following seems to express the essence of a paraphrase. It
is to restate in your own words the ideas of another that are
contained in a short passage. An important point to remember
is that you must make the way in which you convey these
ideas, not just the words, your own. So, in describing the
myth you choose, you should convey the same story, but do so
in a way that does not duplicate the textbook and is
distinctively your own.

The second part of the question is asking you to describe
the myth's function in society: why is this particular myth
important for this society and what role does it play in this
society? This type of description might be termed an

"analytical description." It is not just asking you to
retell the story, but to go further and give an account of
how these nonliterate people make use of the myth so your
reader can understand both the myth and the society. In
order to do this you might consider describing the nature of
the society, and how this myth is appropriate for such a
society. Or you might look at the structure of the society,
and see if this structure is reflected in the myth.

PART NINE   PROJECTS FOR DEVELOPING RELIGIOUS EMPATHY

1. This chapter discusses the important role that dreams play
   in the religions of many nonliterate peoples. In cultures
   such as that of the Naskapi, dreams are used to predict
   the future or teach the hunter. Today, we often look to
   dreams not to predict the future, but to reveal aspects of
   ourselves normally hidden from our conscious minds. But
   our dreams may also be a door through which we can gain
   entry into the consciousness of earlier, nonliterate
   peoples, and develop empathy for their way of life. As
   Jung stated:

       One cannot afford to be naive in dealing with dreams.
       They originate in a spirit that is not quite human,
       but is rather a breath of nature - a spirit of the
       beautiful and generous as well as of the cruel goddess.
       If we want to characterize this spirit, we shall
       certainly get closer to it in the sphere of ancient
       mythologies, or the fables of the primeval forest, than
       in the consciousness of modern man. [4]

   To get in touch with this primeval spirit, and to
   understand the role that dreams have played in nonliterate
   cultures, you might want to keep a dream journal. Such a
   journal is easy to begin, but it does require some
   discipline and preparation. First, you should put a
   notebook and a pen by the side of your bed, where you can
   easily reach it. You will want to write down your dreams
   as soon as you awake. Next, every night before you fall
   asleep, tell yourself that you will remember at least one
   dream and will write it down. Repeat this to yourself a
   number of times. Then, when you wake up in the night or
   in the morning, get in the habit of immediately writing

down whatever you can remember of your dreams. This is important, since waiting even one or two minutes can result in much of the dream being forgotten. Just write down everything you can remember. Finally, later in the day or evening, reread the description and jot down any thoughts or reflections you have on the dream. Why might you have dreamt what you did? Could your dream be a reflection of any events or concerns in your life? How might a person from one of the cultures in this chapter have interpreted your dream? Would you accept this interpretation? Why or why not?

2. The author of the textbook states that myths are not to be found only in ancient religions, but also in contemporary life. Try to think of examples of myths that we Americans believe in or use. You might first want to review the different definitions or theories of myths presented in the textbook, in order to help you decide what is and is not a myth. Are the four criteria of Laurie Hanko useful? Or do you find that the approach of Kees W. Bolle has more validity? Using the definition you choose, what examples of myths can you find? Are any of these myths actually stories of "gods"? How many of the myths are related to stories of the beginnings of our country, and the form of our government, as Bolle suggests? How many relate to our jobs or careers? In what way do these myths contribute to the self-image we have as Americans? Do you think we are aware of these as myths, or are myths only myths when we do not consciously question them?

3. Story-telling appears to be making a comeback in our culture. At day-care centers and at open-air festivals, one can find story-tellers practicing their art. Many ethnic groups are promoting story-telling as a way to hand on their heritage to future generations. Even on the radio, story-tellers such as Garrison Keillor are attracting new audiences.

Among nonliterate societies story-telling is crucial. Cultures which lack a written language must pass on their stories by telling them orally, and must develop ways to do so with great accuracy. However, in telling and re-telling the story, each teller shapes the story by his skill and to his needs. As G. S. Kirk has argued:

Every time a poem or a tale is sung or recited,
unless there is a written version - or in rare
cases an oral one so sacrosanct that it is known
virtually by heart - its form is slightly altered.
. . . [This] is a generalization that seems valid
wherever it can be checked among non-literate
societies, whether primitive or not, and one which
seems to accord with several distinct human
capacities and limitations. . . they will be varied
in some degree on virtually every occasion of
telling, and the variations will be determined by
the whim, the ambition or the particular thematic
repertoire of the individual teller, as well as by
the receptivity and special requirements of the
particular audience. [5]

Listen to friends who you might consider to be good story-
tellers as they spin their tales. What sort of stories do
they tell? How do they structure their stories to keep
the audiences interest? When you hear them tell the same
story a number of times, how do they change the tale? Do
they alter the story according to the audience? Do these
observations give you any insights into the role of story-
telling in a culture without written language (or
television)?

ANSWER KEY TO SELF-TEST

b) Multiple choice

1. b	6. c
2. a	7. a
3. c	8. b
4. d	9. d
5. d	10. a

c) True-False

1. T	6. F
2. F	7. F
3. T	8. F
4. T	9. T
5. T	10. T

Notes

[1]Rudolf Otto, The Idea of the Holy, 2nd ed., trans. John W. Harvey, (Oxford: Oxford University Press, 1950) 12-14.

[2]G. S. Kirk, Myth: Its Meaning and Functions in Ancient and Other Cultures (Berkeley: University of California Press, 1973) 34-40.

[3]Max Weber, The Sociology of Religion, 4th ed. trans. Ephraim Fischoff (1922; Boston: Beacon Press, 1964) 1.

[4]Carl Jung, "Approaching the Unconscious," Man and His Symbols, ed. Jung and M.L. von Franz (Garden City, NY: Doubleday, 1964).

[5]G. S. Kirk, Myth: Its Meaning and Functions in Ancient and Other Cultures (Berkeley, CA: University of California Press, 1973) 73-74.

Chapter 2

RELIGIONS OF
ANCIENT CITY-STATES

PART ONE   LEARNING OBJECTIVES

Doing these exercises, in conjunction with reading the
textbook, should help you to achieve many of the following
objectives. Read them and see how many you already have
mastered; then study the following terms and concepts, and
work through the exercises. After you have completed all the
exercises, review the objectives again.

You should be able to:

1. Delineate the major differences between the cultures of
   nonliterate peoples and of ancient city-states, and
   between the religious expressions of nonliterate peoples
   and of ancient city-states.

2. Define and differentiate between a "city-state" and a
   "nation".

3. Know and write down a brief outline of ancient Egyptian history, and how this history was reflected in Egyptian religious beliefs and practices.

4. Describe the nature and characteristics of Egyptian religion, including being able to describe the major Egyptian deities, some Egyptian religious practices, and the views of the Absolute, and of life after death.

5. Cite some examples of how Egyptian religion influenced the beliefs and practices of other cultures.

6. Give an brief outline of the history of ancient Mesopotamia, and delineate some major differences between the geography, history and culture of Mesopotamia and Egypt.

7. Describe the nature and characteristics of Mesopotamian religion, including the major Mesopotamian myths and deities, some Mesopotamian religious practices and the views of the Absolute and of life and death.

8. Cite some examples of how Mesopotamian religion influenced the beliefs and practices of other cultures.

9. Describe the Athenian festival called the "Panathenaea", and explain some roles this festival and the goddess Athena played in the life of Athens in the Classical Age.

10. Give a brief outline of the history of Greek civilizations from the Minoan civilization up until 404 B.C.E.

11. Describe and analyze the development of Greek religion from the Minoan-Mycenaean Age to the Golden Age of Athens, focusing especially on the Greek view of the Absolute and use of rituals and symbols.

12. Relate at least three Greek myths, and discuss the significance of these myths.

13. Explain how some Greek philosophers viewed the traditional Greek religion, and the development and nature of the Hellenistic worldview.

14. Discuss and analyze the Aztec religion, including being able to discuss the Aztec view of the gods, and man's

relationship to the gods. You should also be able to describe the major Aztec rituals.

15. Discuss and analyze the religion of the Incas, including being able to discuss the Inca beliefs in the gods and other manifestations such as the huacas.

16. Describe at least one major Inca religious ritual.
17. List and explain some common features of the religions of city-states, and give illustrations of these features from the religions studied in this chapter.

18. Discuss and write about the idea of immortality, analyzing how this concept was addressed in Greek, Egyptian and other cultures.

PART TWO   TERMS AND INDIVIDUALS

A) Terms and Concepts

city-states   nations

EGYPT

pyramid	hieroglyphics
Horus	Isis
Osiris	Amon-Re (Ra)
Aton	Hathor
Mayet (Maat)	Sakhmet
Bast	ankh
Seth	ka
ba	akh (ikhu)

MESOPOTAMIA

ziggurats	cuneiform
Gilgamesh	Sumer
Akkad	Damuzi
Inanna	An
Enlil	Ninhursaga
Enki	Sin
Shamash	Ishtar
Tiamat	Apsu

Marduk   Damuzi
Tammuz   Ereshkigal
Nirgal   land of Kigal
Anunnaki

GREEK

Acropolis   Parthenon
Athena   Panathenaea
Erichthonios   peplos
Minoan civilization   Mycenaean civilization
Zeus   Poseidon
Hades   Hera
Artemis   Aphrodite
dike   ate
arete   moira
mystery religions   Dionysus
Orpheus   maenads
Demeter   Persephone
Eleusinian mystery cult   Hellenistic period
Mt. Olympus   Stoics
Mithras   Gnosticism
gnosis

AZTECS

Tenochtitlan   Huitzilopochtli
Chichimec   Coatlicue
Tlaloc   Tlazolteotl
Xochiquetzal   Tonatiuh
Tezcatlipoca   The Stone of the Sun
Quetzalcoatl   Aztecs

INCAS

Coriancha   Inti
Viracocha   Incas
huacas   virgins of the sun
Situa   yahuar sanco
huayaya

B) Individuals

Pharaoh Cheops   Pharaoh Akhenaton
Queen Hatshepsut   Ptolemy I

Hammurabi	Agamemnon
Homer	Pericles
Pythagoras	Plato
Socrates	Aristotle
Epicurus	Lucius Apuleius
Valentinus	Montezuma
Atahualpa	Huascar

C) Texts

Egyptian Book of the Dead	Enuma Elish
The Epic of Gilgamesh	Metamorphoses

D) Individuals and Terms From Other Traditions

Alexander The Great	Julius Caesar
Hyksos	Hittites
Philistines	Maimonides
Herodotus	Paul
Hernando Cortes	Francisco Pizaro
Pedro Sancho de la Hoz	fetish

PART THREE   GUIDED REVIEW

1. Two differences between the cultures of nonliterate people and of city-states is that the later had _____ and _____.

2. Many of the religions you studied in this chapter influenced major world religions of today. For example, scholars believe that Judaism was influenced by the religions of both _____ and _____.

3. Whereas a "city-state" refers to _____ _____, the term "nation" refers to _____ _____.

4. The earliest Egyptian civilization began along _____ _____.

5. The writing system used by the Egyptians is called
_____, which could be described as _____
_____.

6. The king of the gods for the Egyptians was _____,
who was symbolized by a _____.

7. The goddess who was symbolized by a woman's body with the
head of a cow was called _____. She was the
_____.

8. The unity of the Egyptian worldview emphasized an
important aspect of life in Egypt: _____.

9. The Egyptian temple represented _____.
Among the duties of the priests at a temple might be to
_____, to _____, and to
_____.

10. For the Egyptians, Osiris symbolized _____
_____.

11. The soul for the Egyptians was comprised of the _____,
the _____, and the akh or ikhu. The akh could be
defined as _____.

12. The process that bound together the ka and the body is
called _____.

13. After one died, one would appear for judgement before
_____.

14. King Amenhotep IV is noted for _____.
This change was reversed by his son, _____.

15. The structures similar to pyramids that were built in
Mesopotamia are called _____.

16. The writing system used in Mesopotamia was _____.
This was done with _____.

17. After about 4000 B.C.E. the culture that dominated
Mesopotamia was that of the _____.
The people who gained control around 2300 B.C.E. were called
_____.

18. Jacobsen argues that the earliest Mesopotamian gods were perceived as _____.   In the third millennium, however, the gods were seen as _____. Finally, during the second millennium, gods were given roles as _____.

19. One of the best known deities was Ishtar, who was the goddess of _____.

20. Two famous Babylonian epics are _____ and _____.

21. The Babylonian creation myth explains the creation of heaven, earth and man by the story of _____ _____ _____.

22. In the story that bears his name, the hero Gilgamesh journeys under the sea in search of _____. While he is there, Utnapishtim tells him a story about _____.

23. One of the messages of the Gilgamesh story seems to be that man _____.

24. At the top of the ziggurat one would find _____ _____.

25. The most famous building atop the Acropolis in Athens is the _____.   It was a temple to the goddess _____.

26. The important festival called the Panathenaea was celebrated in Athens once every _____ years. During the course of this festival, the statue of Athena would receive a new _____.

27. The great civilization on the island of Crete is usually called the _____ civilization.

28. The Mycenaean civilization on the mainland had a famous king called _____, who led the Greeks in a war against _____.

29. Many of the early Greek gods seem to be similar to the gods found in _____.

30. The greatest distinction between Greek gods and humans was that humans were _____ and the gods were _____.

31. In the hierarchy of the Greek gods, the greatest god was _____. His wife was _____.

32. Zeus was associated with the concept of _____, which separated man from the animals. However, the Greeks also believed that man could be overcome by _____ sent by the gods.

33. During the offering of animal sacrifices to the Greek gods, often the _____ of the animal were used for divination. By eating some of the flesh of the animal, the participants were _____.

34. The god of wine and intoxication was _____. His followers were often women, who, according to some reports, engaged in the practices of _____ _____.

35. Orphism stressed values and practices such as _____ _____.

36. The myth concerning Demeter and Persephone involves a story that explains _____.

37. The question that Socrates put to Euthyphro was _____ _____.

38. In the thought of Plato and Aristotle one can notice a growing separation between _____ and _____.

39. The Hellenistic Period begins with _____ _____, and ends with _____ _____.

40. The most common symbol of Mithraism was _____ _____. This cult was a favorite with soldiers because it emphasized _____ _____.

41. Gnosticism emphasized _____.

42. The chief deity of the Aztecs was Huitzilopochtli, the god of _____. The Aztecs believed that he needed to be fed _____.

43. The female goddesses of the Aztecs symbolized the powers of _____.

44. The Stone of the Sun could be described as _____ _____.
It symbolized _____.

45. Since it was believed that the sun could only be kept alive with sufficient supplies of blood, the Aztecs held that human life depended on _____.

46. The heart of the Inca Empire was located in _____ _____.

47. The chief of the Incas was the representative of _____. The Coriancha was _____ _____.

48. The early god of the Incas was _____. He was symbolized by _____ carried by the priests in a basket.

49. This earlier god was superseded by _____, who, it was believed, created _____.

50. Unusual appearances in rocks or plants, or the city of Cuzco itself, were seen by the Incas as _____.

51. The Situa festival involved three stages: a)_____ _____,
b)_____,
and c) _____.

52. One common feature of the city-state religions was that _____, _____ and _____ were seen as interdependent.

53. The problem for a human being in a city-state society was to _____.
This was done by _____.

54. Socrates claimed that philosophy was, at least in part, a type of training for _____.

55. The Egyptians and the Incas both preserved the human body after death in an attempt to _____.

PART FOUR   ANALYZING TEXTS

Below are two texts that were not in the textbook. Both texts, however, do contain ideas and concepts with which you should be familiar after reading the textbook. Read each text carefully, and try to analyze each by answering the following questions: What are the main ideas in the text? What viewpoint or viewpoints might the author of the text represent? Is it possible to identify the specific thinker, discipline, movement, tradition or work from which the text derives? What intellectual, literary, social, cultural or historical influences are reflected in the text? For each of your conclusions, try to point to specific evidence in the text (e.g. terms, ideas, arguments, writing style, etc.) which supports your conclusion. Be careful that your conclusions do not exceed the evidence upon which they rest.

TEXT ONE

Let us reflect in another way, and we shall see that there is great reason to hope that death is a good; for one of two things - either death is a state of nothingness and utter unconsciousness, or, as men say, there is a change and migration of the soul from this world to another. Now, if you suppose that there is no consciousness, but a sleep like the sleep of him who is undisturbed even by dreams, death will be an unspeakable gain. . . . Now, if death be of such a nature, I say that to die is gain; for eternity is then only a single night. But if death is the journey to another place, and there, as men say, all the dead abide, what good, O my friends and judges, can be greater than this? . . . What would not a man give if he might converse with Orpheus and Musaeus and Hesiod and Homer? . . . Wherefore, O judges, be of good cheer about death, and know of a certainty, that no evil can happen to a good man, either in life or after death.[1]

TEXT TWO

How manifold are thy works!
They are hidden before men,
O sole God, beside whom there is no other.
Thou didst create the earth according to thy heart.

Thou didst make the distant sky in order to rise
    therein,
In order to behold all that thou hast made . . .
The world subsists in thy hand,
Even as thou hast made them.

When thou hast risen they live,
When thou settest they die;
For thou art length of life of thyself,
Men live through thee.[2]

PART FIVE   SELF-TEST

A) Definitions and Descriptions - Write your own definition or
description of each of the following terms. After completing
the self-test, check your answer with the definition or
description given in the textbook.

1. arete _____

_____
_____.

2. cuneiform_____

_____
_____.

3. Quetzalcoatl _____

_____
_____.

4. city-states _____

_____
_____.

5. Parthenon _____

_____
_____.

6. maenads _____

_____

_____.

7. huacas _____

_____

_____.

8. ba _____

_____

_____.

9. Marduk _____

_____

_____.

10. Aton _____

_____

_____.

B) Multiple Choice

1. The story of Utnapishtim in the Mesopotamian Epic of
   Gilgamesh is a story of

   a. The creation by the gods of an ideal person.
   b. A great flood, and how a man, his family and the
      animals were saved in an ark.
   c. A man who searches for immortality, but loses it to
      a serpent.
   d. How man first discovered fire.

2. The Egyptian leader who appears to have worshiped only one
   god was

   a. King Tutankhamen.
   b. King Cheops.
   c. King Akhenaton.
   d. King Vidor.

3. The chief god of the Aztecs was

   a. Huitzilopochtli.
   b. Tlaloc.
   c. Tonatiuh.
   d. Tezcatlipoca.

4. Mummification for the Egyptians was supposed to bind the body to what aspect of the soul?

   a. ba
   b. ikhu
   c. akh
   d. ka

5. The Greeks believed that when men acted irrationally they were being touched by

   a. moira.
   b. dike.
   c. ate.
   d. arete.

6. Which of the following is not one of the acts of the Inca Situa festival?

   a. The Emperor orders the city purged of all foreign influences.
   b. Inca knights go to battle throughout the city.
   c. Participants eat or wear a kind of dough.
   d. The emperor is sacrificed to the sun god in order to ensure a good harvest.

7. The earth mounds covered with bricks that were built in ancient Mesopotamia are called

   a. ziggurats.
   b. pyramids.
   c. kofun.
   d. Damuzi.

8. In the very important Egyptian myth of Isis and Osiris, their son who was symbolized by a falcon was

   a. Hathor.
   b. Horus.
   c. Aton.
   d. Seth.

9. Which of the following gods or goddesses was not the central figure in one of the older, pre-Hellenistic Greek mystery religions?

   a. Dionysus
   b. Orpheus
   c. Demeter
   d. Mithras

10. Which of the following would not be considered a religion of an ancient city-state?

   a. The religion of the Cherokees
   b. The religion of the Aztecs
   c. The religion of the Incas
   d. The religion of the Athenian Greeks

C) True-False

T F   1. The great festival that was held every four years in Athens in honor of the goddess Athena was the Olympic Festival.

T F   2. In the Egyptian religion, when the god Mayet went to judge you and weighed your heart in a balance, the lighter your heart, the better you had been in life.

T F   3. The Mesopotamian epic entitled the Enuma Elish is a myth of creation.

T F   4. An animal who was accorded great honor in Egypt was the cat.

T F   5. Socrates disagreed with Epicurus, and held that the soul was not immortal.

T   F   6. The notion of a city-state refers to a
                  form of government, and not to a territory.

T   F   7. A favorite religion among Roman soldiers was
                  the mystery religion of Mithraism.

T   F   8. The writing system that the ancient
                  Egyptians used is called cuneiform.

T   F   9. The Aztecs sacrificed many people because
                  they believed the blood and hearts of the
                  victims kept the sun alive.

T   F   10. The pattern of weather and flooding in Egypt
                  was much more unpredictable than the pattern
                  in Mesopotamia.

PART SIX   ESSAY AND DISCUSSION QUESTIONS

1. What is distinctive in the religious beliefs and practices
   of the ancient Egyptians?

2. Imagine that by some miracle of time travel you could
   actually live in either ancient Egypt during the Old
   Kingdom Period or ancient Mesopotamia of the second
   millennium. What would be the differences in how each
   society saw man, his place in the universe and his
   relation to the gods? In which society would you prefer
   to live? Why?

3. Describe the Greek view of the gods. ' Why might the Greeks
   have had so many gods?

4. Compare the early Greek ideas of the Absolute to the ideas
   of the Absolute during the Hellenistic Period. What are
   the chief differences and what are the main similarities?

5. Both the Mesopotamian myths and the Greek myths deal with
   the actions of the gods and how these actions affect human
   life. To what extent, and in what specific ways, do the
   myths from the two traditions attempt to justify for
   humans the actions and ways of the gods?

6. Explain how the Aztecs viewed the universe, man's role in
   the universe, and his relation with the gods.

7. Describe how the Absolute might be manifest in the day to day life of the Incas.

8. Delineate, in your own words, the basic features of both religions of nonliterate people, and city-state religion. How would you compare these two types of religions?

PART SEVEN   CONFRONTING QUESTIONS AND ISSUES

The city-state religions of ancient Egypt, Greece and Mexico have today ceased to be a "live option", to use William James's phrase, for most of the people living in these countries. The ancient faiths have long ago been supplanted by Christianity, Islam or a modern faith in man himself. It is very difficult, therefore, to say that there are issues confronting these ancient city-state religions. And yet, as the chapter in the textbook made clear, they have had an important influence on more contemporary world religions and on Western culture. In many senses, these are the roots of our heritage. Scholars continue to study these cultures and religions, uncovering in the sands of time and the sands of the desert new clues on what they believed and who we have become. These scholars, however, must try to answer certain questions in order to understand the clues they uncover.

It is often easier to discover new texts or monuments from one of these ancient city-states, than to understand the consciousness that lies behind the artifact. Many of the rituals from these cultures, and the beliefs that underlie the rituals, appear to us as irrational. When, for example, you read in the textbook that the Aztecs killed many humans every day in order to feed their blood and hearts to Huitzilopochtli, you may feel horror and revulsion. But you may also feel that their belief that this must be done in order to make sure that the sun rises everyday lacks any kind of mental clarity or well thought out order. Such beliefs do not "make sense" to us. Nevertheless, it is too easy to dismiss the Aztec worldview as totally irrational. These beliefs must have made some sort of "sense" to the Aztecs, for they oriented their lives around them. In addition, part of the task of a scholar of religion is to discover and communicate the order that lies beneath such beliefs.

Imagine, then, that you are a scholar studying an ancient city-state religion. Assume for the moment that you are studying the Aztecs. Consider how you would deal with the following questions, and how your answers to these questions might influence your study and be influenced by your study. How is it possible for you, a person of the Twentieth century, to understand a way of living and thinking such as that of the Aztecs? Does such a way of thinking possess a type of reason or order, or is it merely an irrational type of thought? If it does possess a sort of rationality, is there still such a difference between the way the Aztecs, for example, looked at the world and the way we look at the world that we can never understand their way of thinking? Is the implication, therefore, that some cultures will be closed forever to our understanding?

PART EIGHT   AN ESSAY FOR DEEPER CONSIDERATION

Essay Question

Compare the views of immortality in the city-state religions of Egypt and Mesopotamia.

Tips for Answering

Some essay questions will ask you to compare two ideas or things; some essay questions will ask you to compare and contrast. You may find that some of your professors draw a distinction between the tasks of "comparing" and of "contrasting". For some people, to compare is to find similarities, and to contrast is to find divergences. Some of the essay questions in this book should be read in this way. The above essay question, however, is using the word "compare" in a different manner. Here "to compare" means to examine two (in this case) concepts in order to discover how they are alike and how they are different. A comparison between Japanese and American management styles would not just tell you how they are alike, but would also point up where they differ. The essay assignment, therefore, is to draw out for your readers both the differences and the similarities in how these two cultures viewed the problem of immortality.

An interesting and insightful comparison between two things or ideas will probably not be a simple comparison. For example, if you are comparing Japanese and American management you might find that in some respects they are the same, but in other respects they are different. You would be analyzing the larger question into smaller questions, or points (in this case, "management structure", "decision-making process", "group dynamics", etc.). To prepare for a comparison of the Egyptian and Mesopotamian views of immortality, you might want to list the points for comparison. Such points, for instance, could include each religion's view of the gods, of the human soul, of the nature of human existence, and of the after-life. There are certainly others you might want to list. In listing each point you might discover that the two religions are quite close in how they see some points, and quite different in how they view others.

Once you have broken down the larger issue, you need to decide how you are going to integrate these individual points into a unified essay. In general, there are two ways to structure a comparison essay: by <u>block</u> or by <u>point</u>. To compare by block, in this case, would mean to discuss first, point by point, the Egyptian view of immortality. Then, after concluding an analysis of the Egyptian view, you would discuss, point by point, the Mesopotamian view. It would be important, of course, when you are discussing the Mesopotamian view, to refer back and contrast this view to the Egyptian view discussed earlier. To compare by point, on the other hand, would mean to discuss first the Egyptian view of the gods, and then the Mesopotamian view of the gods. Subsequently, you would discuss in tandem their views of the soul, and so on. This method means alternating constantly from one religion to the other. Both methods have their strengths and weaknesses; which is best for you to use will depend on your writing style and your arguments. In both cases, however, you would want to end your essay by summarizing your conclusions and discussing the implications of these conclusions for our view of these two cultures.

PART NINE   PROJECTS FOR DEVELOPING RELIGIOUS EMPATHY

1. The city-states described in this chapter of the textbook
   have ceased to exist. The art and the culture that they
   produced, however, still exists and continues to excite
   our imaginations. This is especially true of the art and
   architecture of Greece. Zeus, Dionysus and Athena all
   come alive in the Greek art (or Roman copies of Greek art)
   that has been preserved. Much of the art from Greece has
   been installed in museums throughout Europe and in
   America. This preservation has not been without
   controversy; many Greeks believe that their art was
   plundered from their country and should be returned to
   them. Whatever position one takes on this issue, it does
   seem clear that the museums have helped preserve and
   restore much of this art. It is through Greek art that
   many of us can most directly enter into the world of the
   Greeks.

   If you are in a city fortunate enough to have a collection
   of Greek art, take an afternoon to visit and view the
   collection. (If you do not have access to a collection of
   Greek art, you might want to examine pictures of Greek art
   in a history of world art in your library. Just bear in
   mind that a picture is only a faint reflection of the
   original.) Take your time to stroll the gallery, examine
   the objects and read the explanations concerning each
   object. Is some of the art familiar to you? Are any of
   the statues or paintings representations of gods or heroes
   discussed in this chapter? What seems to be the way in
   which humans are portrayed in the art? Is there a
   difference in the way men and women are portrayed? If the
   collection is comprehensive, notice the way in which man
   is portrayed in the Archaic, the Classical and the
   Hellenistic works. What are the differences in the
   portrayals? What does this tell us about Greek culture
   during these three periods?

2. A further project involving Greek art (or the art of any
   of the other city-states) requires some drawing. When you
   are in the museum, find an object that interests you and
   that is in some way related to the religions you have read
   about in this chapter. For example, you might be
   interested in a statue of the Greek god Zeus, or a

painting on a vase of the god Dionysus. After you have selected an object, do the following: First, make a careful sketch of the object. When you are drawing the object, try to be aware of the proportions of the objects and how it is constructed. Second, go to the library and try to read about objects of a similar nature. What is their place in the history of Greek art and civilization. Third, write down a brief response in which you consider how the object illuminates the culture that produced it. If you find this helpful, you might get in the habit of keeping a combination sketch-note book for museum trips. Drawing an object often makes us more aware of the structure of the object, and the technique of the artist.

3. Every culture has a slightly different view of immortality. One of the best ways to study how a culture views death and the search for immortality is to examine how it treats its dead. Most people in our society take for granted the practice of burying the dead in cemeteries. However, the way in which we view cemeteries is a fairly recent phenomenon. The history of cemeteries is a fascinating subject. Go to a good reference encyclopedia and read the article on cemeteries. What were some of the different reasons for the popularity of cemeteries? How would you compare the Nineteenth century interest in cemeteries to our own view?

Then visit one of the older cemeteries in your town. Observe the graves from different historical periods. Can you notice differences in the style of the tombstones? Can you pinpoint the different styles, and the rough time periods when each style was in vogue? What do the various styles of tombstones (or crypts) and the messages on the tombstones tell us about the view of death and the search for immortality during each period? What do the most recent tombstones tell you about our view of death today?

ANSWER KEY TO SELF-TEST SECTION

B) Multiple Choice

1. b   6. d
2. c   7. a
3. a   8. b
4. d   9. d
5. c   10. a

C) True-False

1. F   6. F
2. T   7. T
3. T   8. F
4. T   9. T
5. F   10. F

Notes

[1]Plato, "Apology," The Works of Plato, ed. Irwin Edman, trans. Benjamin Jowett (1928; New York: The Modern Library, 1956) 87-88.

[2]"Hymm to the god Aton," J. H. Breasted, The Dawn of Consciousness (New York: Charles Scribner's Sons, 1934) 284-286.

Chapter 3

HINDUISM

PART ONE   LEARNING OBJECTIVES

Doing these exercises, in conjunction with reading the
textbook, should help you to achieve the following
objectives. Read them and see how many you already have
mastered; then study the following terms and concepts, and
work through the exercises. After you have completed all the
exercises, return to this section and review the objectives
again.

You should be able to:

1.Discuss the pre-Aryan Dravidian civilization, what is known
   about this culture and its religious practices, the Aryan
   invasion, and the resulting synthesis of the Aryan and
   Dravidian religious traditions.

2. Name the main groups of Hindu scriptures that were produced during the Vedic and Epic Periods, and describe their nature and relations to each other.

3. Describe the nature and characteristics of Vedic religion, including describing the major Vedic deities and worship.

4. Analyze the development of Hinduism from Vedic religion to the Upanishads, including a discussion of the development of different beliefs and practices during these periods.

5. Discuss the doctrine of Brahman-Atman as it is presented in the Upanishads, and, in particular, what this doctrine says about the nature of man, and man's relation to the Universe and the Absolute.

6. Name the six schools of Hindu philosophy, and give a brief description of the basic positions of each school.

7. Describe the system of social stratification known as "varna", and how the ideas of "karma" and "samsara" are used in Hinduism to justify this system.

8. Explain the central problem that Arjuna faces in the Bhagavad Gita, and delineate and illustrate each of the four ways to moksha.

9. Describe the Four Goals of Life, the Four Stages of Life and the Four Ways to Salvation, and explain how each might function in the life of a Hindu.

10. Refer to specific texts from the Hindu scriptures in order to analyze and illustrate the fundamental characteristics of Vedic religion, Brahmanism, Upanishadic Hinduism and the approach of the Bhagavad Gita.

11. Show how Hinduism has developed since the ninth century C.E. in reaction to new influences and new challenges, and recognize the major Hindu thinkers from this period.

12. Discuss and write about the Hindu Worldview; in particular, the Hindu view of The Absolute, the universe, the human role in the universe, the fundamental problem and resolution for human beings, community and ethics, history, rituals and symbols, and other religious traditions.

13. Cite and discuss at least three issues that confront and challenge contemporary Hinduism.

14. Define the concept of reincarnation, analyze how this concept was expressed in Indian and other cultures, and discuss the problem of how evidence could be produced to support the existence of reincarnation.

PART TWO   TERMS AND INDIVIDUALS

A) Terms and Concepts

Dravidian people   Aryan people
varna   Indra
Varuna   Rta
Yama   Prajapati
Vishnu   Shiva
Brahman   devas
asuras   caste
soma   surya
Mitra   rishis
Rhudra   Agni
Brihaspati   Brahmins
Atman   Brahman
tat tvan asi   prakriti
maya   saguna Brahman
nirguna Brahman   moksha
kalpa   reincarnation
shruti   guru
smirti   purusha
Vedanta   Advaita Vedanta
Samkya   Yoga
Vaisheshika   Nyaya
Advista   Purva-Mimamsa
dharma   samsara
Shudras   Vaishyas
Kshatriyas   Krishna
jnana yoga   karma yoga
bhakti yoga   raja yoga
brahmacharya   kama
artha   samadhi
shraddha rites   Brahma
Parvati   Kali

Durga   Ganesh
Nandi   tantrism
Shaivism   Vaishnavism
Lakshmi   Radha
Rama   Sita
Moguls   Brahmo Samaj
Arya Samaj   untouchables
satayagraha   ahimsa
sat-chit-ananda   upanayana rite
puja

B) Individuals

Yajnavalkya   Uddalaka
Svetaketu   Kapila
Sankara   Patanjali
Gautama   Kanda
Jaimini   Arjuna
Ram Mohan Roy   Debendranath Tagore
Ramakrishna   Dayananda Sarasvati
Swami Vivekananda   Rabindranath Tagore
Mohandas K. Gandhi   Sri Auribindo
Sarvepalli Radhakrishnan

C) Texts

Vedas   Rig-Veda
Yajur-Veda   Sama-Veda
Artharva-Veda   Brahmanas
Upanishads   Vedanta Sutra
Bhagavad Gita   Laws of Manu
Ramayana   Yoga Sutra

D) Individuals and Terms From Other Traditions

Jains   Mahavira
Siddhartha Gautama   Buddhism
Plato   Immanuel Kant
Nanak   Kabir
Socrates   St. Thomas
Pythagoras

PART THREE   GUIDED REVIEW

1. The earliest Indian civilization for which we have evidence is that of _Dravidian_ .   Based on archeological evidence, this civilization could be described as _advanced urban and religious_ .

2. Beginning around 1000 B.C.E. a large group of nomadic people began to migrate into India. These people were called the _Aryans_ , which means _noble people_.

3. These invaders honored their gods by _sacrificing animals_ .

4. According to some scholars this conquest of one people by another may have been the origin of the system of social stratification known as _varna (color)_. This predated the more rigid system of social stratification that is usually known as the _castes_ .

5. The earliest Hindu scriptures are collections of text called the _Vedas_ , which means in English _scriptures_.

6. The most important of the four collections is known as the _Rig-Veda_ . It could be described as _praise of Indra, considered the most important deity of the hymns._
Rig-Veda, Soma-Veda, Yajur-Veda, Athora-Veda

7. The hymns of the Vedas are addressed to a great variety of gods. However, among the more important gods were:
   a. _Indra_ , the god of storm, thunder and war.
   b. _Varuna_ , the sky god and the protector of moral order.
   c. _Rita_ , the moral order which underlies the the Universe.
   d. _Manu_ , the first man and the keeper of the dead.
   e. _Agni_ , the god of fire and the sacrifice.

8. In order to relate more directly to the gods, the participants in the sacrifice might drink a beverage called _soma_ .

9. The group of texts called the Brahmanas were _commentaries and manuals_ on the Vedas. The Brahmanas represent a change from the Vedas in that they _are explanations of sacrifices, the second part of the shruti - sacred writings_

smiti - tales remembered, then written
shruti - sacred writings
Vedas - the oldest part of the shruti
Brahmanas - the second part, explanations of sacrifices,
Aranyakas - later parts of the shruti

B.C.E
Before Common Era

81

10. The thinkers whose insights are recorded in the Upanishads are termed ___Vedanda___. Many scholars believe that these thinkers came from castes rebelling against ___rigid Brahmin control of all life.___.

11. The texts called the Upanishads were written in the time period from ___c. 800 ___ to ___300 BCE___.

12. Central to many of the Upanishads is the search for a unity or permenance in the midst of the changing totality of things. For many of the Upanishadic thinkers the permanence they found was called the _____ or _____.

13. The Absolute Reality which is the ground of all things and which transcends all things is called in many of the Upanishads ___Brahman___. The subjective force which is equated with this Reality is called ___Atman___.

14. For Hinduism, Brahman can be viewed in two ways: either as ___nirguna Brahman___, the personal Absolute with attributes, or as ___saguna Brahman___, the impersonal Absolute which transcends all attributes.

15. Hindu scriptures can be classified into two categories: ___Karma___, which means _____ and ___samsara___, which means _____.

16. The Samkya school (Samkhya)? was a dualistic school of philosophy that believed there were two realities in the universe, ___Prakriti___, and ___Purusha___.

17. The greatest thinker of the Advaita Vedanta school was ___Shankara___. He argued that the world of appearence is ___avidya___, while the one true Reality is ___Maya___.

18. The other four schools of Hindu philosophy are _____, _____, _____ and _____.

19. The process of cycles of reincarnation that could stretch over many lifes is called _____. This process is governed by the moral law of action and reaction which is called the law of _____.

20. The four major groups within the caste system are
_____, _____, _____ and
_____. A fifth group who were literally
"outside the caste system" were _____.

21. In the Bhagavad Gita Krishna explains to Arjuna that
there are four ways to obtain release: the way of _____,
the way of _____, the way of _____, and
the way of _____.

22. Hinduism allows it adherants to choose from among four
different goals of life: _____, _____,
_____ and _____.

23. Hinduism believes that there are four stages in the life
of an upper-caste male Hindu; these four stages are
_____, _____, _____
and _____.

24. According to karma yoga, the most important duty for a
Hindu male householder is _____. On the
other hand, among important duties for women would be
_____.

25. Literally thousands of deities are worshipped by
contemporary Hindus, but three deities are the most popular:
_____, _____ and _____.

26. The god Krishna is held to be an avatar of _____.

27. The book that contains the precepts and moral codes which
all Hindus are expected to follow is _____.

28. The Hindu reformer, Ram Mohan Roy, in rejecting
established Hindu beliefs such as polytheism, and in
rejecting Hindu customs such as infanticide of females, was
influenced by _____.

29. The important modern Hindu leader who preached the power
of love, and fought for social justice and Indian
independence was _____.

30. The problem that the Aryans had in describing the forces
of the universe was _____. Many Hindu
leaders addressed this problem by holding that it was better
to _____ than to _____.

31. While the labels of "polytheism" or "monotheism" may appear to be appropriate for Hinduism, the distinctive attitude of Hinduism towards the Absolute is the belief that behind all phenomenon lies _ONE God_____.

32. Many more Hindus prefer to worship deities such as Kali or Krishna, rather than deities such as Brahma, because they are more _intimidating or representative_
Krishna - chariot driver; Brahma - the ultimate reality, creator

33. Compared to the Middle Eastern view of the universe, the Hindu view is more _complicated and yet tolerant_

34. Hinduism rejects the view that humans are only their physical bodies; for Hinduism the body is but a costume for ____the soul____.

35. The human problem for Hinduism is alienation from the Absolute. This alienation occurs both when ___Karma___, and through ___caste___.

36. If for Hinduism the human problem is alienation from the Absolute, then the solution for humans is ___harmony with the absolute_.

37. While Hindus have great respect for all animals, it is of special merit to express compassion for the _cow_____.

38. The Hindu view of history is a _repeating cycles_ view.

39. Religious worship and rituals in Hinduism can be either ___individual___ or ___congregational_.

40. Recently, relations in India between Hindus, Muslims and Sikhs have been ___violent_____.

41. There is a tension in modern India between the old ways and the new. Three issues that modern Hindus must face and attempt to answer are _____,' _____ and _____.

42. In the Bhagavad Gita the Lord Krishna assures the young warrior Arjuna that he can neither _be killed____ or _become a beggar___.

43. The idea that after a person dies his soul will be reborn in a different body is termed ___reincarnation___.

44. The cycle or succession of states of existence that an individual goes through is termed _whool of life_.

45. The two major types of evidence for the occurence of reincarnation are _____ and

_____.

PART FOUR   ANALYZING TEXTS

Below are three texts that were not in the textbook. The texts, however, do contain ideas and concepts with which you should be familiar after reading the textbook. Read each text carefully, and try to analyze each by answering the following questions: What are the main ideas in the text? What viewpoint or viewpoints might the author of the text represent? Is it possible to identify the specific thinker, discipline, movement, tradition or work from which the text derives? What intellectual, literary, social, cultural or historical influences are reflected in the text? For each of your conclusions, try to point to specific evidence in the text (e.g. terms, ideas, arguments, writing style, etc.) which supports your conclusion. Be careful that your conclusions do not exceed the evidence upon which they rest.

TEXT ONE

Higher than this is Brahman. The Supreme, the Great
Hidden in all things, body by body,
The One embracer of the universe-
By knowing Him as Lord men become immortal.

I know this mighty person
Of the colour of the sun, beyond darkness.
Only by knowing Him does one pass over death.
There is no other path for going there.

Than whom there is naught else higher,
Than whom there is naught smaller, naught greater,
The One stand like a tree established in heaven.
By Him, the Person, this whole world is filled. [1]

TEXT TWO

   Those who fixing their minds on Me worship Me, ever
earnest and possessed of supreme faith - them do I
consider most perfect in <u>yoga</u>.
   But those who worship the Imperishable, the
Undefinable, the Unmanifested, the Omnipresent, the
Unthinkable, the Unchanging and the Immobile, the
Constant,
   By restraining all the senses, being even-minded in
all conditions, rejoicing in the welfare of all
creatures - they come to Me indeed [just like the
others].
   The difficulty of those whose thoughts are set on the
Unmanifested is greater, for the goal of the
Unmanifested is hard to reach by embodied beings.[2]

TEXT THREE

What sin we have committed against an intimate, O
Varuna, against a friend or companion at any time, a
brother, a neighbour, or a stranger, that, O Varuna,
loose from us.

If like gamblers at play we have cheated, whether in
truth or without knowing, all that loose from us, O God.
So may we be dear to thee, O Varuna. [3]

PART FIVE   SELF-TEST

A) <u>Definitions and Descriptions</u> - Write your own definition
or description of each of the following terms, individuals or
texts. After completing the self-test, check your answer
with the definition or description given in the textbook.

   1. dharma _____
_____
_____.

2. Shaivism _____
_____
_____.

3. Laws of Manu _____
_____
_____.

4. nirguna Brahman _____
_____
_____.

5. Ram Mohan Roy _____
_____
_____.

6. karma yoga _____
_____
_____.

7. Brahmins _____
_____
_____.

8. Vedas _____
_____
_____.

9. Sankara _____
_____
_____.

10. Atman _____
_____
_____.

B) Multiple Choice

1. According to many of the Upanishads the Ultimate Reality
   is

   a. Prakriti
   b. Maya
   c. Brahman ✓
   d. Brahma

2. The term in Hinduism for the organization of society on
    the basis of color, which predated the more rigid
    stratification of later periods, is

    a. Varna ✓
    b. Veda
    c. Varuna
    d. Caste

3. The god of fire, which was very important for the Vedic
    sacrifice, is named

    a. Agni ✓
    b. Indra
    c. Brahma
    d. Rta

4. Which of the following is not included among the list of
    the four goals in life?

    a. Kama - pleasure.
    b. Artha - material success.
    c. Bhakhti - devotion. ✓
    d. Dharma - duty to ones caste.

5. Based on the text, which of the following would seem to
    be the least troubling problem for contemporary Hinduism?

    a. The demand by seperate religious groups for their own
       political units.
    b. How to adjust the Hindu views on the role of women.
    c. How to relate orthodox views to modern secular views.
    d. How to reconcile the Hindu view of the cosmos to the
       Big Bang theory. ✓

6. Which of the following statements is probably not a true
    statement about the Aryan people?

    a. The name Aryan means "noble people".
    b. The Aryans had a highly advanced urban civilization. ✓
    c. The Aryans honored their gods by sacrificing animals.
    d. Many Aryan practices are reflected in the Vedas.

7. The lowest group within the caste system, unable to even
    hear the Vedas being read, was the

    a. Vaishyas
    b. Brahmins
    c. Shudras ✓
    d. Kshatriyas

8. Which of the following best describes the gurus of the
    Upanishads?

    a. They were priests who officiated at sacrifices.
    b. They were thinkers who taught about the highest
            reality. ✓
    c. They were fortune tellers.
    d. They were founders of the six Hindu philosophical
            schools.

9. The Hindu philosophical system attributed to Kapila,
    which argues that the universe is made up of two radically
    different types of reality is

    a. Advaita Vedanta
    b. Nyaya
    c. Purva-Mimamsa
    d. Samkya ✓

10. The famous nineteenth century Hindu mystic who had an
    absolute devotion to the goddess Kali, but saw Allah,
    Jesus, Krishna and all dieties as manifestations of one
    God was

    a. Ramakrishna ✓
    b. Sri Aurobindo
    c. Radhakrishnan
    d. Rabindranath Tagore

C) True-False

T (F)   1. Hinduism, like Judaism and Islam, rejects the use
           of images in worship.
T (F)   2. Those Hindu writings which are seen as the direct
           revealed word are termed "smriti".

T F   3. One of the earliest Indian civilizations
             was that of the Dravidians, who lived in large
             cities with underground plumbing.

T F   4. Two doctrines that were at the center of Gandhi's
             thought were those of satyagraha and ahimsa.

T F   5. While the Upanishads have as their goal the
             uniting of the atman with the Brahman, not all of
             the Upanishads preach an absolute monism.

T F   6. Many scholars believe that the Brahmanas and the
             Upanishads grew out of the same movement, since
             both de-emphasis the role of the sacrifice.

T F   7. The movement called Arya Samaj, founded by
             Dayananda Sarasvati, was important in the history
             of modern Hinduism because it tried to embrace
             many elements.
             from Christianity and the West.

T F   8. According to Hindu myth, the first man to die,
             Yama, became the keeper of the dead in the
             afterlife.

T F   9. In the Bhagaved Gita Krishna urges Arjuna to not
             lay down his arms, but to enter the battle and
             fight as a warrior.

T F   10. According to the Advaita Vedanta school of
             Sankara, the world is made up of many particular
             things, ultimately understandable as atoms.

PART SIX   ESSAY AND DISCUSSION QUESTIONS

1. Hinduism offers its believers a choice of four goals in
   life. Two of these goals are the pursuit of pleasure, and
   the pursuit of commercial or political success, goals not
   often associated with a religious life. What might be
   some advantages of offering people a choice among goals in
   their life? What might be some of the drawbacks?

2. What evidence does Hinduism offer in favor of the existence of the atman? Do you find the evidence convincing? What might be the most serious challenges to this theory of the atman?

3. Compare and contrast the views of the Absolute contained in the "creation hymm" from the Rig Veda, and in the quote from the Chandogya Upanishad.

4. How would you characterize Hindu responses to the Western influence since the early 1800's? What responses appear to have best meet the challenges of Western influence, and why? Back up your agrument by using specific examples from the text.

5. Given the wide range of practices and beliefs included in what is commonly termed "Hinduism", do you think using the term "Hinduism" is helpful or unhelpful? If you think the term should be used, what criteria determines whether a belief or practice is "Hindu"? If you argue that the term is misleading, what terminology would you employ and why?

PART SEVEN   CONFRONTING QUESTIONS AND ISSUES

The author of the textbook isolates three issues that confront contemporary Hinduism. One of these issues is how Hindus, as he puts it, "will adjust their views on the changing roles of women." Women are becoming college educated, are following business careers and are demanding a role in choosing their own husbands. Yet the overall status of women in traditional Hindu society was, and in many ways still is, very low. In liberating themselves from some of the roles they were assigned in the past many Hindu women base their positions on Western ideas and thinkers. Many, however, also try to ground their positions in their own heritage; that is to say, the practices and ideas of Hinduism itself.

Imagine that you are a Hindu woman who wants to fashion a role for herself as a woman, a role other than that prescribed by The Laws of Manu. To what textual tradition, school of thought or thinker within the traditions of Hinduism might you turn to find the basis for a more equal

role for women? What specific ideas or viewpoints in that
tradition offers the basis for a new status for Hindu women?
What would be the new roles for women?

PART EIGHT   AN ESSAY FOR DEEPER CONSIDERATION

Essay Question

Analyze the meaning and role of "reincarnation" as
revealed in the quotation from the Bhagavad Gita in the
textbook. What is the view of the relation between soul and
body underlying this quote? What evidence could be given in
support of these views of the soul and body, and of
reincarnation? What evidence could be given against these
views?

Tips For Answering

The term "analyze" is used in various ways by different
people. In general, however, to analyze means to break
something down into smaller parts in order to better
understand the whole. An analysis of the question of whether
capital punishment is just may reveal that three or four
different questions are involved. For example, you might
find that the larger issue can not be addressed before you
become clear on your definition of "justice." This would
appear to indicate that you are being asked to break down the
larger question of the meaning of reincarnation as revealed
in the quote into smaller, more specific questions.

This question can be broken down into three somewhat
smaller questions: 1)What is the view of "reincarnation" is
this quotation? 2)What is the view of the soul and the body
in this quotation, and how does this view serve as a basis
for the view of reincarnation? 3)What evidence can be given
in support of such views? It might be helpful to attack each
part of the question seperately when you are researching and
writing your first drafts. While the third part of the
questions almost definitely needs to be answered last, you
might want to address either the first or the second part of
the question in the first part of your essay. That is to
say, you might first examine the relation between the soul
and the body, and demonstrate how this view leads to a theory

of reincarnation. Or, you might first look at the belief in
reincarnation, and then whow how it relateds to a particular
view of the soul and the body.

In answering this essay question make sure that you define
for your readers how you, at each moment in your essay, are
defining the significant terms. For example, terms such as
"reincarnation", "soul" and "body" need to be defined. How
is the Bhagavad Gita defining these terms? Is this a
definition you are using yourself?

PART NINE   PROJECTS FOR DEVELOPING RELIGIOUS EMPATHY

1. When you read the textbook and study this guide the names
    and terms in the ancient Indian language of Sanskrit may
    seem unfamiliar and strange. Yet Sanskrit and English are
    languages that both have a common root: a now lost
    language called Proto-Indo-European. Many of the Sanskrit
    terms you have studied are cognates with English words.
    For example, the Sanskrit term "Trimurti" (meaning the
    Vedaic trinity of the gods Brahma, Vishnu and Shiva) has
    the same part "tri" (three) as the English word
    "tricycle".

    The American Heritage Dictionary of the English Language
    has an appendix which is a list of Indo-European roots.
    If you have a copy of this dictionary, or if the library
    has a copy, try the following: Look up the English words
    "video", "right" and "firm" in the dictionary. At the end
    of the citation for each word will be its Indo-European
    root. For each word look up the root in the Appendix.
    What Sanskrit terms that you already know are related to
    these common English words? How has the form of the word
    seemed to change over time and between languages? Can you
    discover any other English cognates of Sanskrit terms?

2. Many cities and universities have museums of art or
    anthropology which contain collections of Indian art. You
    may already be familiar with one in your area, either
    through trips for an art history class or through going on
    your own. If you are not sure if such resources exist
    near you, the reference librarian at your college or
    university library should be able to show you reference

books that list the museums in the United States and
detail their collections. Your instructor might know of
any collections of Indian art near you.

If you are fortunate enough to be near a museum with a
collection of Indian art, get together with a friend and
take a trip to the museum. Notice whether there are any
objects from the early Dravidian civilization, perhaps
clay seals, or sculptures of the human figure. What do
these pieces tell you about the civilization that produced
them? What do they tell you about the physical nature of
the Dravidians. Next, see whether any works are
identified as being of the Gupta Period. How do these
works differ from the earlier works? If there are statues
of any of the Hindu gods, how are they portrayed? What
aspects of the Hindu view of the Absolute, of man and of
the universe can you see reflected in these works? If
there any more recent Indian works of art in the
collection to what extent do these works reflect Hindu
ideas and values? To what extent do they reflect ideas
and values from other cultures?

3. In 1893 Swami Vivekânanda came to the United States to
    represent Hinduism at the World Parliament of Religions in
    Chicago. Since this time many representatives of Hinduism
    have journeyed to the United States to teach and to start
    religious communities. Vivekânanda himself organized a
    number of Vedantic centers in the United States. These
    centers, named after Vivekânanda's teacher, are part of
    the Ramakrishna Mission.

    If you feel comfortable with the idea, you might think
    about arranging a visit to a Ramakrishna Mission, a yoga
    center or some other Hindu group in your area. You might
    want to first research the groups in your area, and find
    out some information on their beliefs and practices. You
    may feel more comfortable visiting with one or two
    classmates, rather than just by yourself. Contact the
    group that you are interested in visiting prior to your
    actual visit. Explain that you are taking a course in
    World Religions, and your visit would be in order to
    complete a class project. While you would like to
    understand more about Hinduism, and the teachings of this
    particular branch, you should also empahsize that you are
    not seeking to join the group, or become an adherent. If

the members of the community do not feel comfortable with
your stance, than you might want to suggest that you not
visit.

If the community is open to having a number of you visit,
observe their practices and ask questions, then try to
model the role of the religious scholar. Notice what are
the beliefs of the group, and what are the practices.
Which of the Hindu traditions that you have studied seem
to have most influenced this community? Have any of the
beliefs and practices been changed for the Western
audience? How so?

ANSWER KEY TO SELF-TEST SECTION

B) Multiple Choice

1.	c	6.	b
2.	a	7.	c
3.	a	8.	b
4.	c	9.	d
5.	d	10.	a

C) True-False

1.	F	6.	F
2.	F	7.	F
3.	T	8.	T
4.	T	9.	T
5.	T	10.	F

Notes

[1]Svetâsvatara Upanishad, III. 7-9, R. E. Hume, trans., in A Sourcebook in Indian Philosophy, ed. Sarvepalli Radhakrishnan and Charles A. Moore, (Princeton, N. J.: Princeton University Press, 1957) 90-91.

[2]The Bhagavadgîtâ, XII: 1-5, trans. Sarvepalli Radhakrishnan (New York: Harper & Row, 1973) 291-293.

[3]Rg Veda, V: 85, trans. Edward J. Thomas, in A Sourcebook in Indian Philosophy, ed. Sarvepalli Radhakrishnan and Charles A. Moore (Princeton, N. J.: Princeton University Press, 1957) 29.

Chapter 4

BUDDHISM

PART ONE   LEARNING OBJECTIVES

Doing these exercises, in conjunctions with reading the
textbook, should help you to achieve many of the following
objectives. Read them and see how many you already have
mastered; then study the following terms and concepts, and
work through the exercises. After you have completed all the
exercises, review the objectives again.

You should be able to:

1. Understand how some religious belief systems have formed
   around a central historical figure and personality, and
   what issues arise when scholars attempt to interpret
   stories of the person's life.

2. Outline the life of Siddhartha Gautama, the Buddha, and

79

discuss the significance for Buddhism of the central events in his life.

3. Explain the central teachings of the Buddha, and analyze the significance of his teachings. In particular, you should be able to explain the Buddhist teachings of The Four Noble Truths, <u>pratitya-samutpada</u>, The Middle Path, <u>Samsara</u> and <u>Nirvana</u>, and questions which do not tend to edification.

4. Name the main divisions into which Buddhist scripture is divided, and describe the nature of each group of writings and how they came to be written down.

5. Analyze the development of Buddhism in India from the death of the Buddha to the appearance of the Mahayana Schools. In particular, you should be able to talk about the role of King Asoka, and the respective positions of the Theravda and Mahayana branches of Buddhism.

6. Give a brief description of at least two Indian Mahayana Schools, and explain how their positions differed from earlier Buddhism.

7. Show how Buddhism changed after its arrival in China, and name at least four Chinese Buddhist schools and give a brief description of their basic positions.

8. Describe the development of Buddhism in Japan, and name at least five Japanese Buddhist schools and give a brief description of their basic positions.

9. Give the main outline of the history of Buddhism in Tibet.

10. Compare and contrast the forms of Buddhism that originated and developed in India, China, Japan and Tibet, focusing particularly on how Buddhism adapted to a variety of cultures, and how the Buddhist realization was expressed in variety of forms.

11. Discuss and write about the Buddhist Worldview; in particular, discuss and write about the Buddhist view of The Absolute, the universe, the human role in the universe, the fundamental problem and resolution for human beings, community and ethics, history, symbols and life after death.

12. Understand how Buddhism has had an influence in America and Europe, and what issues and challenges confront Buddhism in this new environment.

13. Define the concept of Buddhist meditation, illustrate the stages of Buddhist meditation, and show how the Buddhist use of meditation differs from meditation in other religious traditions, and illustrate.

PART TWO   TERMS AND INDIVIDUALS

A) Terms and Concepts

Bodh Gaya
The Four Passing Sights
Mara
The Middle Path (Middleway)
Sangha
The Ten Precepts
Tathagata
Mahayana
tanha
jhana
no-Self (anatta)
samsara
Nirvana (Nibbana)
Sthaviras
Maitreya Buddha
Hinayana
Avalokitisvara (Kwan Yin)
Sarvastivadas
Haimavatas
Vatsiputriyas
Dharmaguptikas
Sautrantikas
Caityakas
Yogacara school
Hua-Yen School
Suchness
Amitabha Buddha (Amida)
Ch'an (Zen)
Ryôbu Shinto
mudras

Buddha
The Bo Tree
Sakya clan
The Four Noble Truths
Dharma
Bhikkus
Theravada
dukkha
The Eightfold Path
skandhas
pratitya-samutpada
karma
Mahasamghikas
arahat
Tusita heaven
bodhisattva
Mahasasakas
sarvam asti
dharmas
pudgala
Kasyapiyas
Bahushrutiyas
Madhyamika School
T'ien-T'ai School (Tendai)
Vairochana Buddha (Vairocana)
Pure Land School (Ching-t'u)
Kuan-yin Bodhisattva (Kwannon)
Three Kingdoms Period
mantra
mandala

"Namu Amida Butsu"   Pure Land Sect (Jôdo)
Hôzô Bosatsu   dhyana
Lin Chi Sect (Rinzai)   Ts'ao-tung Sect (Sôtô)
satori   koan (kung-an)
Nichiren Sect   "Namu Myôhô-renge-kyô"
tantric Buddhism   Tara
kalachakra   puja
Nyingmapa   Gelugpa
lama   the Dalai Lama
Soka Gakkai   Kômeito
anicca   Trikaya
Nirmanakaya   Dharmakaya
Sambhogakaya   karuna
Buddhist Churches of America Jôdô Shinshû (True Pure Land)
prajna (panna)   samadhi
kasina

B) <u>Individuals</u>

Queen Maya   Siddhartha Gautama (Sakyamuni)
King Suddhodana   Yasodhara
Rahula   Alara Kalama
Uddaka Ramaputta   Sojata
Ananda   Mahakasyapa
Nagasena   King Milinda (King Menander)
Malunkyaputta   Kisogotami
King Mahapadma   King Asoka
King Kanishka   Chandragupta
Nagarjuna   Vasubhandhu
Mou Tzu   Chi Kai
Fa-tsang   Bodhidharma
Emperor T'aejong   Emperor Kimmei
Soga clan   Empress Suiko
Prince Shôtoku Taishi   Saichô (Dyengo Daishi)
Kukai (Kôbô Daishi)   Ryônin
Hônen Shônin (Genku)   Shinran
Nichiren   Padma-Sambhava
U Nu   S. W. R. D. Bandaranaike
Thich Tri Quang   Thich Thien Minh
Makiguchi Tsunesaburo   D. T. Suzuki
Tsultrim Allione (J. Ewing) Buddhaghosa

C) <u>Texts</u>

Tripitaka   Vinaya Pitaka
Sutta Pitaka   Abhidharma Pitaka

Mahavibhasa   jatakas
The Disputation of Error   Lotus Sutra (Saddharm-Pandarika
Avatamsaka Sutra   Sikyavativyuha
Lankavatara Sutra   The Heart Sutra
Red Annals   Mijjhima Nikaya
Visuddhimagga

D) Individuals and Terms From Other Traditions

Brahmin   Ksyatriya
brahmacarya   Alexander The Great
Neo-Confucianism   Mao Tse-tung
mu   mudang
Shinto   Amaterasu
Bon   Hatha Yoga
Shakti cults   Karl Marx
Marxism   Thomas Merton

PART THREE   GUIDED REVIEW

1. Bodh Gaya is a site of pilgrimage for Buddhists from
around the world because _____.

2. One difference between Hinduism and Buddhism is that
Buddhism begins with _____.

3. The name of the person who would become the Buddha was
_____, and he was later known as
_____.

4. The four sights that Siddhartha saw were _____,
_____, _____, and
_____.

5. After Siddhartha decided that he could not find what he
sought from his teachers he embarked on a course of _____
_____. At the last
moment he realized that this path was _____.

6. The Four Noble Truths that the Buddha first taught in the
Deer Park at Sarnath were the Noble Truth concerning
_____, concerning _____, concerning
_____, and concerning
_____.

7. When one is initiated into Buddhism, one takes a vow to take refuge in the _____, the _____, and the _____.

8. Ordinary human existence is <u>dukkha</u>, which the Buddhists take to mean _____
_____.

9. The Buddhists, unlike most of the Hindu schools, did not believe man had a _____. Instead, they believed that man was comprised of the Five _____.

10. Both the Hindus and the Buddhists believed that life was a cycle of rebirths, termed _____. This cycle was governed by the power of _____.

11. When this cycle of death and rebirth is brought to an end, the Buddhists term this _____, which means literally _____.

12. The collected Buddhist scripture is gathered together in the _____, which means _____
_____. These are the _____,
the _____, and the _____.

13. The two major branches of Buddhism are the _____, and the _____.

14. A being who delays his own entry into Nirvana in order to help all sentient beings attain Nirvana is termed a _____. The type of Buddhism that would use this term in this manner is _____ Buddhism.

15. The Madhyamika School, usually associated with the philosopher _____, taught that _____
_____.

16. The Yogacara School, whose greatest thinkers were the brothers _____ and _____, taught that _____
_____.

17. Buddhism began in China around the year _____.

18. Pure Land Buddhism believed that a person should look to
_____ for help, and should say the name
_____.

19. The monk who brought Ch'an Buddhism to China from India
was _____. The world "Ch'an" itself means
_____.

20. The native religion of Korea was called _____, and
that of Tibet was termed _____.

21. Buddhism was important in Japan, in part, because the
importation of Buddhism also resulted in the arrival in Japan
of _____ and _____.

22. Saichô was the founder in Japan of the _____
sect, while Kukai founded the _____ sect.

23. Kukai believed that at the absolute level joining the
real world of ideas with it phenomenal counterpart is
_____ Buddha, also known as _____.

24. Three means that Shingon uses to express the Absolute are
_____, _____, and _____.

25. Hônen did not believe that one could reach salvation
through ones own efforts, but instead had to rely upon
_____.

26. Shinran broke with Buddhist tradition in that he _____
_____ and he _____.

27. Shinran viewed human nature as _____
_____.

28. The Sanskrit word for "meditation", dhyana, came to be
used for the name of a sect of Buddhism: _____, in
Chinese and _____, in Japanese.

29. The two major branches of this form of Buddhism were the
_____ branch, which emphasized _____
_____, and the _____
_____ branch, which emphasized _____
_____.

30. The Zen Buddhist practice which takes its name from the Chinese word for "case study" is today known in Japanese as _____.

31. Two examples of art forms that have been influenced by Zen Buddhism are _____ and _____.

32. The Japanese Buddhist prophet who emphasized reliance only on the Lotus Sutra was _____.

33. The native religion of Tibet is _____.

34. The form of Buddhism common in Tibet is called _____ Buddhism.

35. Three practices that are stressed in Tibetan Buddhism are:
    a) mantras, which are _____.
    b) mandalas, which are _____.
    c) mudras, which are _____.

36. The two major branches of Tibetan Buddhism are the _____, who wear _____ hats, and the _____, who wear _____ hats.

37. The Gelugpa sect finds replacements for the head of their orders through _____.

38. The Buddhist politician who combined Buddhism and socialism in Burma was _____.

39. The Buddhist left-wing political party in Japan is the _____.

40. The famous Japanese teacher of Zen Buddhism who did much to popularize Zen in the West was _____.

41. The Buddhist doctrine that all things are impermanent is called in Pali _____.

42. While it might not be correct to say Buddha did not believe in gods, it is probably correct to say that he viewed them as _____.

43. For Buddhism, the central human problem is that of
_____, and the central message of Buddhism is how
to _____.

44. The central Buddhist social virtue is _____,
which is usually translated as compassion for all sentient
beings.

45. While Buddhism did not believe in the Atman, it did
believe in _____.

46. For Theravada Buddhism, the three stages in meditative
process are:
  a) _____.
  b) _____.
  c) _____.

PART FOUR   ANALYZING TEXTS

   Below are three texts that were not in the textbook.
   The texts, however, do contain ideas and concepts with
   which you should be familiar after reading the textbook.
   Read each text carefully, and try to analyze each by
   answering the following questions: What are the main
   ideas in the text?   What viewpoint or viewpoints might
   the author of the text represent? Is it possible to
   identify the specific thinker, discipline, movement,
   tradition or work from which the text derives? What
   intellectual, literary, social, cultural or historical
   influences are reflected in the text? For each of your
   conclusions, try to point to specific evidence in the
   text (e.g. terms, ideas, arguments, writing style, etc.)
   which supports your conclusion. Be careful that your
   conclusions do not exceed the evidence upon which they
   rest.

TEXT ONE

   Subhuti: How is perfect wisdom marked?
   The Lord: It is marked with the non-attachment of space.
      It is, however, no mark, nor does it have one.
   Subhuti: Would it be possible for all dharmas to be

found by the same mark by which the perfection of
wisdom is to be found?

The Lord: So it is, Subhuti, so it is. The mark by
which perfect wisdom exists, through just that mark
all dharmas also exist. Because all dharmas are
isolated in their own-being, empty in their own-
being. In that way all dharmas exist through the
mark by which perfect wisdom exists, i.e. through
the mark of emptiness. . . [1]

TEXT TWO

"Already, when a person has faith that he will be
saved by the power of the Original Vow of Amida Buddha,
and that it is possible for him to be born in the Pure
Land, and already, when by believing this, there arises
in him the heart of Faith which is the foundation for
the mental activity such as calling-out to and reciting
the Name of Amida Buddha (Nembutsu), already previous to
this time Amida Buddha has conferred on us the Grace
which brings us to His salvation."

"The Vow of Amida Buddha does not discriminate
between the old and the young, the virtuous and the
wicked. You must understand that in Amida Buddha's Vow,
the essential key to receiving salvation is Faith, and
only Faith. The reason for this is because Amida
established His Vow precisely to try and save those
people who suffer from violent cravings and intense,
grave evil."

"Henceforth, for those people who have faith in the
Original Vow, with the exception of invoking Amida's
Name, even good actions and good works are unnecessary,
since there is nothing which surpasses the excellence of
the Nembutsu. I do not even fear the sins which I have
committed and am committing, since there is no sin or
evil which is great enough to obstruct the fulfilling of
Amida Buddha's vow. [2]

TEXT THREE

Misery only doth exist, none miserable.
No doer is there; naught save the deed is found.
Nirvana is, but not the man who seeks it.
The Path exists, but not the traveler on it.[3]

PART FIVE   SELF-TEST

A) Definitions and Descriptions - Write your own definition
or description of each of the following terms, individuals or
texts. After completing the self-test, check your answer
with the definition or description given in the textbook.

1. dharmas _____
_____
_____ .

2. Dharmakaya _____
_____
_____ .

3. Theravada _____
_____
_____ .

4. Nichiren sect _____
_____
_____ .

5. Hôzô Bosatsu _____
_____
_____ .

6. Sangha _____
_____
_____ .

7. Buddha _____
_____
_____ .

8. koan _____
_____
_____ .

9. mantra _____
_____
_____ .

10. anicca _____

_____

_____ .

B) Multiple Choice

1. The school of Nagarjuna which taught that all dharmas are Empty (sunya) was the

   a. Sarvastavada school.
   b. Yogacara school.
   c. Madhyamika school.
   d. Theravada school.

2. The term for the Buddhist teaching of no-Self is

   a. anicca
   b. dukkha
   c. anatta
   d. ahimsa

3. Which of the following is not one of the Four Noble Truths?

   a. The truth concerning dukkha.
   b. The truth concerning the origin of dukkha.
   c. The truth concerning the cessation of dukkha.
   d. The truth concerning the continuance of dukkha.

4. The Japanese school that would make use of the koan is the

   a. Pure Land school.
   b. Zen school.
   c. Nichiren school.
   d. Tendai school.

5. Which of the following sights is not one of the Four Passing Sights that the Buddha saw?

   a. a sick man.
   b. a dead man.
   c. a poor man.
   d. an old man.

6. Which of the following is <u>not</u> one of the bodies of the Buddha mentioned in the <u>Trikaya</u> theory?

   a. Sambhogakaya
   b. Nirvanakaya
   c. Nirmanakaya
   d. Dharmakaya.

7. A Buddhist does <u>not</u> take refuge in which of these?

   a. God
   b. the Teaching
   c. the Community
   d. Buddha

8. If one was looking in the Tripitaka for the rules for monks and nuns, one would probably look in

   a. the Abhidharma Pitaka.
   b. the Vinaya Pitaka.
   c. the Sutta Pitaka
   d. the Whole-wheat Pita.

9. In what century did Buddhism probably arrive in China?

   a. first century C.E.
   b. first century B.C.E.
   c. second century C.E.
   d. second century B.C.E.

10. The Chinese sect that taught the theory of One-in-All was

   a. Hua-Yen sect.
   b. Ch'an sect.
   c. Ching-t'u sect.
   d. T'ien-T'ai sect.

C) <u>True-False</u>

T F   1. The Emperor Asoka sent many missions to various parts of Asia that spread the Buddhist teaching.

T F   2. The historical Buddha began life in India as Sakyamuni.

T F   3. The native religion of Korea is <u>bon</u>.

T F   4. One of the central teachings of Early
                 Buddhism is that only the Self is
                 permanent and unchanging.

T F   5. Shinran broke with Buddhist tradition by
                 marrying and eating meat.

T F   6. Ch'an Buddhism was brought to China by
                 Bodhidharma.

T F   7. The Early Buddhists differed from Hinduism
                 in rejecting the authority of the Vedas.

T F   8. According to Theravada Buddhism a monk who
                 has achieved enlightenment is called a
                 bodhisattva.

T F   9. The Tibetan Buddhist sect called the Gelugpa
                 are called "Red Buddhists."

T F   10. In Buddhism the goal is a state of awakening
                 or enlightenment that is called Nirvana or
                 Satori.

PART SIX   ESSAY AND DISCUSSION QUESTIONS

1. Explain the significance that the story of the life of the
   Buddha would have for a Buddhist.

2. Early Buddhism attacked the belief in any kind of
   permanent Self or Atman. It did, however, retain a belief
   in reincarnation and karma. Explain how Early Buddhism
   could believe in reincarnation but not believe in a Self
   that is reincarnated.

3. Early Buddhism rejected a belief in a Soul. It also held
   that the notions of God and of an after-life are, at best,
   irrelevant. Given these positions should Early Buddhism
   be classified as a religion? Examine arguments on both
   sides of this question.

4. Analyze whether or not Indian Buddhism and Japanese
   Buddhism are so different in their worldviews and
   practices that they should be regarded as two different
   religious traditions. In your analysis consider
   especially the case of Pure Land Buddhism, which appears
   to be radically different from the teachings of the
   historical Buddha.

5. All schools of Buddhism claim to be a "Middleway" or
   "Middlepath". Compare how three schools of Buddhism -
   Indian Theravada Buddhism, one school of Indian Mahayana
   Buddhism and one school of Japanese Buddhism - might stake
   out their claims to being the true Middleway.

PART SEVEN   CONFRONTING QUESTIONS AND ISSUES

   The "Questions and Issues" section of the textbook raises
the question of how well Buddhism can adapt to the modern
world and what role Buddhism can play in modern society. The
answer to this question will depend, it is clear, on many
factors. The attitude of the central government, and indeed
the nature of the central government, in countries such as
China or Cambodia will play a significant role in determining
the future of Buddhism in these countries. Economic
prosperity and material affluence in nations such as Japan
and Taiwan will make the traditional Buddhist virtues of
restraint and non-reliance on material possessions less
attractive. An argument could be made, however, that one of
the most pressing problems facing Buddhism today is the need
to clearly articulate a relevant social philosophy. In an
area of the world with pressing social problems and in which
various forms of Marxism, socialism and capitalism are
competing for the allegiance of the people, what social ethic
does, or can, Buddhism offer?

   Try and grapple with the problem of how Buddhism can offer
a message on a social, and not just an individual, level.
Choose a problem that is a pressing issue for the people of
the world. Examples to consider might be the environment,
the role of women, nuclear proliferation or achieving a more
equitable distribution of the world's resources. Given your
study of Buddhist thought, could Buddhism formulate a social
philosophy to deal with the issue you have chosen? Does
Buddhism have a social dimension, or is it concerned only
with individual salvation? Does Buddhist thought contain

criteria for evaluating social issues (i.e.."what is fair", "what is equitable","what is moral")? If so, what might be these criteria? How could these criteria be applied to the particular issue you are considering?

PART EIGHT   AN ESSAY FOR DEEPER CONSIDERATION

Essay Question

Compare the views of Self (Atman) presented in the Upanishads and in Early Buddhism. Delineate and examine the arguments and justifications given by both sides to support their positions. How would you evaluate the soundness of each side's argument?

Tips for Answering

This essay question asks you to develop your essay by reasoning in ways similar to previous "Deeper Consideration" essays. For example, you are clearly being asked to compare (and contrast) the Upanishadic view of Atman to the Buddhist view of Atman. In order to undertake such a comparison you will have to describe the basic positions of the two traditions as you understand them. In addition, you will have to analyze the positions of each to be able to delineate their arguments. Nevertheless, in one sense, this question is asking you to go beyond merely comparing two positions, or analyzing the significance of each position. It is asking for a critique, or evaluation, of each position. That is to say, you are being asked to lay out the arguments on each side of this issue, and then evaluate which, if either, side is presenting a sound argument or a strong justification.

An argument, in ordinary speech, often means a dispute, or a situation in which two people exchange angry words. But in philosophy and many academic disciplines an argument is a special use of language and reason. Many times when we are speaking or writing we make claims that something is true, or assert that such and such is the case. When we do this we are making assertions, or making truth-claims. When someone advances an argument, however, he or she is not just making assertions. He is also asserting that some of these assertions are reasons for others. That is to say, an argument makes the claim that one or more specific assertions ought to be accepted as true, or probably true, just because certain other statements are true. The goal of an argument, therefore, is to get you to accept one assertion as being true by showing you that other assertions are true. Seen in this way the minimal ingredients of an argument are: 1) at least one statement that is reasoned <u>for</u> (this is the <u>conclusion</u>), 2) at least one statement that is alleged to <u>support it</u> (this is the <u>reason</u>), and 3) some signal that an argument is taking place (the use of terms such as "therefore" or "because").

The above essay question is asking you to present, not just the positions of both traditions, but their arguments. You will need to present not just the conclusions that each side takes, but also what reasons, evidence or justification each gives for believing the conclusion to be true. When you are presenting the argument for each side, you should attempt to do so fairly and objectively. You are also being asked, however, to evaluate the arguments or the evidence. Does the evidence justify the conclusion? When you undertake such an evaluation you will probably argue much more in favor of one of the positions. Make sure that in answering this question you are not just giving your opinion, but are taking a position based on rigorous examination of the arguments. You are taking your own position and backing it up; which is to say, you are advancing your own argument.

PART NINE   PROJECTS FOR DEVELOPING RELIGIOUS EMPATHY

1. The Buddha claimed to have discovered a number of significant truths concerning the nature of human existence, and the path to a resolution of the fundamental human problem. One of these truths was the realization that all composite existence is transitory (<u>anicca</u> in Pali, <u>mûjô</u> in Japanese.) People think there <u>is</u> a stability in their lives that the Buddhists claim does not really exist. If we look closely at ourselves and the world around us we will see impermanence, not stability.

This idea of change is reflected in many Buddhist writings. Consider this poem written by a medieval Japanese Buddhist monk:

When we consider the self, it is like a bubble on the
    water;
After it has burst, there is no one there.

When we reflect on our lives, they are like the
    reflections of the moon;
As unstaying as the rise and the fall of the breath.

Even though we cherish the beneficial forms of gods and
    men;
No one can retain them.

Even though we hate the agony of being hungry ghosts and
    beasts;
After all, these forms are easy to take on. . .

The smelling of scents, the savoring of tastes,
Are for a brief period only.

When the operations of the breath cease,
No functions stay behind in the body.

From far, far back in the distant past
Until today, until this instant,

Because all the things we have thought we wanted
Have not been granted, we suffer.[4]

Try to share the Buddhist way of viewing the world by
examining the impermanence in ourselves and the world.
What within yourself is permanent and unchanging? Is it
your body? Examine how your body changes during the
course of time: you lose skin cells and hair, you lose or
gain weight, you become older and slower. Maybe your
consciousness is permanent? Examine then your thoughts.
Do your thoughts stay still and are they constant? Try
focusing on one thought for a minute or two. Do you
discover that your thoughts are constantly changing,
shifting rapidly from one thought to another which
replaces it? Are you likely to find that the emotions
anymore stable? You might find that the feeling you awake
with only lasts a few minutes. Each feeling is soon
replaced by another feeling. This is the point of the
Buddhist analysis, that when we examine ourselves closely

we see that there is no permanence, only change. Does
this mean that there is nothing here? The Buddhists would
also reject this option. It is not that there is nothing,
just that what there is dynamic and changing. Of course,
many Hindus disagreed with the Buddhists on this point.
For the Hindus there is something permanent that underlies
all the change. When you analyze who you are, do you see
a permanent Self, as the Hindus thought? Whose analysis
seems more accurate?

2. The Buddhist links the idea of impermanence to the idea of
the composite nature of things. Things change because
they are not really objects, but are parts in an
interdependent relationship with a linguistical overlay.
As Nagasena says to King Milinda, the word "chariot" is
nothing but a convenient designation for the axle, banner,
wheel, etc. in a certain causal relationship to each
other. We think we live in a world of objects, but we are
wrong, the Buddhists tell us.

Try one more bit of Buddhist analysis. Choose any object
you can see. What do you mean when you call it an object?
Is it one thing or a group of parts joined together? How
could you analyze it into smaller parts? Now, choose any
one of those smaller parts. Is it not the case that this
part is itself made up of still smaller parts? Do we
still not have a group of parts? Now, you can choose one
of those smaller parts, and start the analysis again. You
can see where this process is leading. Either you must
eventually reach a part so small it can not be sub-
divided, or this analysis must proceed on an infinite
course. The Buddhists claim that this process does reach
an end, when one reaches the smallest possible unit of
time and space (dharmas). Does your analysis lead you to
see the Buddhist point of view? What might we call these
smallest parts today?

3. Much of the Buddhist teaching is expressed in fairly
abstract or analytical thought. It is perhaps for this
reason that Buddhism has always expressed its teaching in
a more concrete manner, art. The story of the Buddhas life
was expressed in sculpture and in painting. Each Buddhist
culture took the same basic motifs and expressed them in a
slightly different manner. Much of this rich harvest of
Buddhist art is available for viewing in this country.

If you are fortunate enough to be near a museum with a
good collection of Asian art, get together with a friend
and take a trip to the museum. Observe if the museum has
art from any of the major countries influenced by
Buddhism: India, Sri Lanka, Tibet, China, Korea, Japan and
the Southeast Asian countries. Which of these collections
contain art with Buddhist figures and themes? How can you
tell if the art is in some sense "Buddhist?" What might
have been the original function of these objects? Can you
find two objects from different countries (for example,
India and China) that deal with the same theme (for
example, two statues of Sakyamuni Buddha or two paintings
of the life of the Buddha)?   What are the differences in
the two objects? What might explain the different
treatments? What aspects of the Buddhist world view can
you see expressed in art?

ANSWER KEY TO SELF-TEST SECTION

B) <u>Multiple Choice</u>

1. c	6. b
2. c	7. a
3. d	8. b
4. c	9. a
5. d	10. d

C) <u>True-False</u>

1. T	6. T
2. F	7. T
3. T	8. F
4. F	9. F
5. T	10. T

Notes

[1]Satasahasrika XLV:119, <u>Buddhist Texts Through the Ages</u>, ed. Edward Conze et al., trans. Edward Conze (New York: Harper Torchbooks, 1964) 153.

[2]<u>Tannishô</u>, words attributed to Shinran Shônin, Chap. 1., unpublished translation by the author, David C. Prejsnar.

[3]Buddhaghosa, <u>Visuddhi-Magga</u>, XVI, <u>Buddhism In Translation</u>, ed. tran. Henry Clarke Warren (1896, New York: Antheneum, 1968) 146.

[4]Ippen Shônin, <u>Betsuganwasan</u>, tran. David C. Prejsnar, "Ippen's View of Time and Temporality in the <u>Betsuganwasan</u>", <u>Jishûshi Kenkyû</u> 1.1 (1985): 6-7.

Chapter 5

text 172-182 / text 259 / text 193

JAINISM, ZOROASTRIANISM, AND SIKHISM

PART ONE   LEARNING OBJECTIVES

Doing these exercises, in conjunction with reading the textbook, should help you to achieve the following objectives. Read them and see how many you already have mastered; then study the following terms and concepts, and work through the exercises. After you have completed all the exercises, return to this section and review the objectives again.

You should be able to:

1. Name the two major orders of Jain monks, and delineate the main points of disagreement between the two orders.

2. Give the life story of the twenty-fourth Tirthankara, Mahavira, illustrating how his life exemplified Jain teachings, and explain how the two major orders differ in

101

presenting the story of Mahavira's life.

3. Name the chief divisions of the Jain scripture, and briefly explain the nature and present status of each of these divisions.

4. Discuss and write about the Jain Worldview; in particular, the Jain view of the Absolute, the relative truth of all views, the universe, the human role in the universe, the fundamental problem and resolution for human beings, rituals and symbols, community and ethics, and other religious traditions.

5. Explain the Jain concept of <u>ahimsa</u>, and critique and evaluate the Jain justification for their belief in <u>ahimsa</u>.

6. Give the life story of Zarathustra, illustrating how his life exemplified Zoroastrian teachings.

7. Summarize the teachings of Zarathustra, especially addressing the question of whether his teachings reflect a monotheistic or a dualistic view of the Absolute.

8. Analyze the development of Zoroastrianism after the death of Zarathustra, focusing especially on the evolving understanding of the Absolute in Zoroastrianism.

9. Discuss and write about the Zoroastrian Worldview; in particular, the Zoroastrian view of the Absolute, the universe, the human role in the universe, the fundamental problem and resolution for human beings, symbols and rituals and life after death.

10. Name at least one forerunner to the founder of the Sikh movement, and illustrate in what sense he anticipated the later Sikh movement and teaching.

11. Give the life story of Guru Nanak, illustrating how his life exemplified Sikh teaching.

12. Discuss and analyze the teachings of Guru Nanak, in particular explaining his view of the Absolute and his view of Hinduism and Islam.

13. Name at least four Sikh gurus who followed Nanak, give a brief outline of their lives, and explain the development of the Sikh movement during their lifetimes.

14. Discuss the view of scripture as it is presented in Sikhism, and consider how this view of scripture compares with the view of scripture in other Indian religious traditions.

15. Discuss and write about the Sikh worldview; in particular, the Sikh view of the Absolute, the human role in the universe, the fundamental problem and resolution for human beings, rituals and symbols, community and ethics, life after death and other religious traditions.

16. Describe the current situation for Sikhs in India, and the problem of relations between Sikhs and other religio-ethnic groups in India.

PART TWO   TERMS AND INDIVIDUALS

A) Terms and Concepts

JAINISM

Jainism	Tirthankaras
Digambaras	Svetambaras
"sky clad"	karma
Rsabhadatta	Devananda
Sakra	ahimsa
householder	Rsabha
moksha	Nirvana
jina	isatpragbhara
Agama	Ardhamagadhi
Parshva	jivas
ajivas	samsara
mohiniya	jnanavaraniya
darsanavaraniya	antaraya
vedaniya	nama
ayu	gotra
gunasthana	puja
Sthanakvasis	satya
steya	bramacarya

aparigraphy   sellekhana

ZOROASTRIANISM

Zoroastrianism   Ahura Mazda
Zoroastrians (Parsees)   daevas
ahuras   Spitama
Vohu Manah   Angra Mainyu
Amesha Spentas   Asha Vahista
Khshatra Vairya   Spenta Armaiti
Hourvatat   Ameretat
Chinvat Bridge   Magi
Sassanians   Manichaeism
Zurvanism   Zurvan
Anahita   Haoma
Mithra   asha
Naozot   sudreh
kusti   dakhma
Sraosha   Uthamna ceremony
dualism   eschatology

SIKHISM

Golden Temple of Amritsar   Adi Granth
Sikhism   Sant
Guru   karma
samsara   Hakum
the Khalsa   Singh
Kesh   Kangha
Kach   Kara
Kirpan   gurdwara
bhais   nihangs
reincarnation

B) <u>Individuals</u>

JAINISM

Mahavira   Trisala
Nataputta Vardhamana   Siddhartha
Indrabhuti Gautama   Jinasena
Haribhadra   Prince Sreyamsa
Rsabha   Chamunda Raya
Ganga Raja

ZOROASTRIANISM

Zoroaster (Zarathustra)   Spitama
Dughdhova   Pourushaspa
King Vishtaspa   Cyrus the Great
Darius   Xerxes
Mani

SIKHISM

Kabir   Nanak
Mardana   Angad
Amar Das   Ram Das
Arjun   Har Gobind
Har Rai   Har Krishen
Teg Bahadur   Gobind Rai (Gobind Singh)
Singh Bhindranwale

C) <u>Texts</u>

JAINISM

Agama   Purva
Anga   Angabahya
Acaranga Sutra   <u>Great Legend</u> (Mahapurana)
<u>The Story of Samaraditya</u>

ZOROASTRIANISM

Avesta   Gathas
Yasna   Visperand
Yashts   Vindedad
Zend-Avesta

SIKHISM

Adi Granth   Japji
Rahat Maryada

D) <u>Individuals and Terms From Other Traditions</u>

Hinduism   Buddhism
Buddhas   Brahmins
Kshatriyas   Shiva
Albert Schweitzer   Brahman-Atman
Vedas   Christian Trinity

Isaiah   St. Augustine (A. Augustine)
Islam   Akbar
Aryan   Dravidian
Upanishads   Ramanuja
Bhakti movement   Sufis
Allah   Nirguna Brahman
Saguna Brahman   Vishnu

PART THREE   GUIDED REVIEW

1. The three heterodox religious traditions, besides
Buddhism, that have been very influential in India are
_____, _____, and
_____.

2. In Jainism the term "Tirthankara" means those who are
_____.

3. _____ was the historical founder of Jainism
and the _____ in the line of Tirthankaras.

4. The two major orders of Jain monks are the
_____ and the _____.

5. The order that rejects the wearing of clothes and does not
allow women to become members of the religious order is
_____.

6. The order that believes that Mahavira was conceived
through an embryo transplant is _____.

7. For some Jains not wearing clothes is important because it
indicates that the monk _____.

8. The name for the Jain cannon, or collection of scripture,
is _____.

9. A cornerstone of the Jain philosophy is that no doctrine
can claim to have _____; however, from some
point of view all doctrines have some _____.

10. The Jains conceive of the universe as be comprised of two
realities: _____ and _____.

11. For Jainism, the "glue" that binds humans to samsara is
_____.

12. _____ is the Jain doctrine of non-
violence and respect for life. The modern Hindu leader who
attributed his practice of non-violence to the Jains was
_____.

13. A religion that began in Persia but today has many
adherents in the Bombay area of India is _____.
In India the followers of this tradition are called
_____.

14. The founder of this movement that began in Persia was
_____, who is also known by his Latin
name of _____.

15. In Zoroastrianism there is a belief in _____,
who is the Wise Lord and God. There is also, however, a
belief in Angra Mainyu, who is _____.

16. Among the scriptures of Zoroastrianism is the
_____, the book of the Law, and the
_____, used to honor the lords.

17. The six intermediaries between God and human beings are
the _____.
18. After death, a person's soul has to cross _____
_____.

19. The ancient Zoroastrian priests who may appear in the
account of Jesus's birth are the _____.

20. _____ developed from the teachings of
Mani, who believed that the universe was _____
_____.

21. The central question in the Zoroastrian view of the
Absolute is whether the good force and the evil force are
_____.

22. Unlike many other religious traditions in India
Zoroastrianism rejects the belief in _____.

23. Among the symbols of Zoroastrianism the most important
one is _____. This is most likely to be found
at the _____, which outsiders must not
enter.

24. The initiation rite into Zoroastrianism that occurs in
the seventh year of a child's life is _____.

25. One of the most unusual aspects of Zoroastrianism is the
ritual treatment of the dead. The body is usually taken to
_____. At this place the body is
_____.

26. One reason that the numbers of Zoroastrians may be in
decline is that in general Zoroastrianism opposes _____
_____.

27. In religious studies, teachings concerning the end of
time or the last things are called _____
teachings.

28. The youngest of the major religions of India is
_____.

29. Many scholars see this Indian religion as an attempt to
_____ Hinduism and Islam. In
fact, it is today a _____.

30. _____ is usually seen as a forerunner of the Sikh
movement in that he _____.

31. The actual founder of the Sikh movement and the first
guru in the lineage of gurus was _____.
32. Nanak is famous for stating that "There is no _____
and no _____", which means that _____
_____.

33. In comparing Nanak's views with that of Hinduism, he
agreed with Hinduism in _____
_____, but he disagreed with Hinduism
in _____.

34. It could be said that the central teaching of Nanak is
that _____.

35. Nanak's view of the human soul and its relation with God is _____
_____ .

36. Nanak saw the Word of God as _____
_____ .

37. Nanak saw five stages in an individual's progress towards God. A brief summary of these five stages would be:
    a) _____ .
    b) _____ .
    c) _____ .
    d) _____ .
    e) _____ .

38. The successor to Nanak and second guru was _____ .

39. The guru who began the construction at Amritsar, and under whom the Sikh order began to grow financially prosperous was _____ , who was the _____ guru.

40. The guru who began to construct the _____ at Amritsar and who was tortured to death by Jahangir was _____ , the _____ guru.

41. Because of what happened to his father, Har Gobind responded by _____ and by
_____ .

42. The tenth and last earthly guru was Gobind Rai. He is better known, however, as _____ .

43. The Sikh ritual called Khalsa could be described as
_____ . The five men who first underwent this ritual were called _____ , which means _____ .

44. Since the death of the tenth guru the only guru for the Sikhs is _____ .

45. The attitude of Sikhism towards the Hindu Brahman and the Muslim Allah is _____ .

46. If one entered a gurdwara, at the center one would probably find _____ .

47. At a <u>gurdwara</u>, one might encounter two different types of Sikh functionaries: _____, who are _____, and _____, who are _____.

48. In India today, many Sikhs are agitating for the creation of _____.

PART FOUR   ANALYZING TEXTS

Below are three texts that were not in the textbook. The texts, however, do contain ideas and concepts with which you should be familiar after reading the textbook. Read each text carefully, and try to analyze each by answering the following questions: What are the main ideas in the text? What viewpoint or viewpoints might the author of the text represent? Is it possible to identify the specific thinker, discipline, movement, tradition or work from which the text derives? What intellectual, literary, social, cultural or historical influences are reflected in the text? For each of your conclusions, try to point to specific evidence in the text (e.g. terms, ideas, arguments, writing style, etc.) which supports your conclusion. Be careful that your conclusions do not exceed the evidence upon which they rest.

TEXT ONE

"O Maker of the material world, thou Holy One! Where are the rewards given? Where does the rewarding take place?" . . . Ahura Mazda answered: "When the man is dead, when his time is over, then the wicked, evil-doing Daevas cut off his eyesight. On the third night, when the dawn appears and brightens up, when Mithra, the god with beautiful weapons, reaches the all-happy mountains, and the sun is rising: then the fiend, named Vizaresha . . . carries off in bonds the souls of the wicked Daeva-worshipers who live in sin. The soul enters the way made by Time, and open both to the wicked and to the righteous. At the head of the Chinvad bridge, the holy bridge made by Mazda, they ask for their spirits and souls the reward for the worldly goods which they gave away here below. Then comes the beautiful, well-shapen, strong and well-formed maid, with the dogs at her sides . . . She makes the soul of the righteous one go up above the Haraberezaiti; above the Chinvad bridge she places it in the presence of the heavenly gods themselves. [1]

TEXT TWO

There is but one God whose name is True, the Creator, devoid of fear and enmity, immortal, unborn, self-existent, great and bountiful.

The True One was in the beginning, the True One was in the primal age.

The True One is, was, O Nanak, and the True One also shall be. [2]

TEXT THREE

Right belief, right knowledge, right conduct - these together constitute the path to liberation.

Belief in things ascertained as they are is right belief.

This is attained by intuition or understanding.

The categories (tattvas) are souls (jiva), non-souls, inflow (asrava) of karmic matter into the self, bondage (bandha) of self by karmic matter, stoppage (samvara) of inflow of karmic matter into the self, shedding (nirjara) of karmic matter by the self, and liberation (moksa) of the self from matter. . .

The points of view (naya) are: figurative, general, distributive, actual, descriptive, specific, and active.

Naya may be distinguished from niksepa. Niksepa is an aspect of the thing itself. Naya is a point of view from which we make some statement about the thing . . .
[3]

PART FIVE   SELF-TEST

A) Definitions and Descriptions - Write your own definition or description of each of the following terms, individuals or texts. After completing the self-test, check your answer with the definition or description given in the textbook.

1. ahimsa _____
_____
_____.

2. the Khalsa _____
_____
_____.

3. Manichaeism _____
_____
_____.

4. Ahura Mazda _____
_____
_____.

5. eschatology _____
_____
_____.

6. "sky clad" _____
_____
_____.

7. Adi Granth _____
_____
_____.

8. bhais _____
_____
_____.

9. dakhma _____
_____
_____.

10. jivas _____
_____
_____.

B) <u>Multiple Choice</u>

1. The Muslim figure who first tried to combine Hinduism and Islam was

   a. Nanak
   b. Mardana
   c. Mahavira
   d. Kabir

2. Which is not one of the five K's of the Singhs?

   a. Comb
   b. Turban
   c. Short pants
   d. Sword.

3. Which of the following religious traditions did <u>not</u> believe in reincarnation?

   a. Jainism
   b. Zoroastrianism
   c. Sikhism
   d. All of the above

4. The Jain scripture of which eleven of the twelve books are still in existence is the

   a. Purvas
   b. Angas
   c. Angabahya
   d. Vedas

5. For Zoroastrians the evil deity is

   a. Ahura Mazda
   b. Vohu Manah
   c. Asha Vahista
   d. Angra Mainyu

6. Which one of the following is not one of the six Amesha Spentas?

   a. Ahura Mazda
   b. Khshatra Vairya
   c. Hourvatat
   d. Asha Vahista

7. Which Sikh guru first took a military stand against the Hindu or Muslim rulers?

   a. Har Gobind
   b. Amar Das
   c. Gobind Singh
   d. Nanak

8. The name of the Jain sect who reject the wearing of clothes is

   a. Digambaras
   b. Svetambaras
   c. Sautantrikas
   d. Sthanakvavis

9. Which of the three religions in this chapter could be considered monotheistic?

   a. Jainism
   b. Zoroastrianism
   c. Zoroastrianism and Sikhism
   d. Jainism and Sikhism

10. Which of the following beliefs did Jainism not share with Hinduism?

   a. Karma
   b. Soul
   c. Reincarnation
   d. Authority of Vedas

C) True-False

T F   1. Jains believe that all statements are relative, and can be seen as true from at least one perspective.

T F   2. Zoroastrianism has both Fire Temples and Towers of Silence.

T F   3. Digambaras sect tells a fascinating story of an embryo transplant.

T F   4. The guards at a Sikh gurdwara are the bhais.

T   F   5. The Indians called the Zoroastrians Parsees,
               because they originally came from Persia.

T   F   6. The Jain concept of non-violence is termed
               satya.

T   F   7. According to Jain belief, the Tirthankaras
               are above the gods.

T   F   8. The hymns of Zarathustra are collection in
               works called gathas.

T   F   9. Nanak rejected any distinction between Hindu
               Brahman and Islam's Allah.

T   F   10. The guru in Sikhism today is Har Gobind.

PART SIX   ESSAY AND DISCUSSION QUESTIONS

1. Define the concept of "ahimsa" and explain its role in
   Jainism. What reasons might Jainism to justify their
   belief in non-violence?

2. Explain the Jain doctrine of the relativity of all views
   (naya). How might the Jains use this doctrine to examine
   and critique the Hindu-Buddhist debate concerning the
   Atman?

3. Examine the question of whether Zarathustra espoused
   monotheism or dualism. How would you define each of these
   terms? Is a middle position between monotheism and
   dualism conceivable?

4. The Problem of Evil is a major issue in monotheistic
   religions: how could evil exist in a world created by an
   omnipotent, good God? How would Zoroastrianism explain
   the existence of evil in the world? Would Zoroastrianism
   have to address the Problem of Evil, and if so, how would
   it address it?

5. Appraise Sikhism as an attempt to transcend the
   distinction between Hinduism and Islam. Did Sikhism
   attempt to unify the two religions, and ,if so, did it
   fail?

6. Compare the Jain and the Sikh view of armed struggle and the use of violence. What are the strengths and weaknesses of each position?

PART SEVEN   CONFRONTING QUESTIONS AND ISSUES

The religions you have studied up until this chapter have all been the dominant religions within their culture. The three religions discussed in this chapter are different; each of the three has, for most of its existence, been a minority religion. In the India of today, all three of these religions claim much fewer participants than either Hinduism or Islam. This fact raises an interesting problem, how can a religious tradition survive when it is a minority belief in a dominant culture?

Imagine that you are writing a survival manual for religions in this difficult position. You will want to consider these three traditions, since in each case it is a minority faith, and yet it has managed to survive with some vigor. How has each of these three traditions managed to survive and prosper? What historical factors have contributed to the survival of each tradition? What approach did each tradition take in order to assure its survival? You might want to consider such factors as organizational structure, clan or tribe loyalty, initiation ceremonies, and political moves. What does your study show you about how religions survive when they do not dominate the culture?

PART EIGHT   AN ESSAY QUESTION FOR DEEPER CONSIDERATION

Essay Question

The three religions discussed in this chapter all take interesting positions in regard to the status of truth-claims. Jainism takes the position that all truth-claims are relative. Zoroastrianism could be interpreted as claiming that there are two radically different first principles in the Universe, one good and one evil. Sikhism could be seen as the attempt to present a valid truth-claim in order to

correct two invalid, but opposing truth-claims (Islam and
Hinduism). In an essay, examine the way in which each
religion makes claims about what is true, and how these
claims illustrate each religions' theory of truth-claims.

Tips For Answering

This is a very complex essay assignment that will require
a great deal of thought and planning. Some suggestions on
how you can tackle this assignment will be discussed shortly.
But the complexity of the issue makes a discussion of another
topic relevant: the thesis statement.

Any good essay needs a clearly formulated and communicated
thesis. But when you are tackling a very complex subject it
is even more crucial to clearly formulate and state your
thesis, or else you, and your reader, run the risk of getting
lost in the essay. A thesis can be defined as the general
point you want to prove or argue for in your essay. In most
essays you will be referring to many specific historical
facts, religious doctrines, or view of scholars. These
particulars should be included in your essay, however, only
because they lend support or clarification to your thesis.
Woody Allen once said he became a better director when he
learned to leave more jokes on the cutting-room floor. In
the same way, too much information or too many arguments can
clutter your essay. You need to understand what major point
you want to prove and then structure your essay so all the
particulars lend support to this thesis.

Before you formulate the thesis for your essay you may
need to do some preliminary brainstorming. One topic you
should consider is the definition of "truth-claim." The
essay question uses this term but does not define it. Many
philosophers use this term, so you might want to consult a
dictionary or encyclopedia of philosophy to become acquainted
with their discussion of the term. The general meaning of
the term, however, is to make a claim that something is true,
or something is so and so. It is to take a position about
what is true, and what is not true.

Begin your answer by breaking the essay question into
smaller units. The first question is "What type of claims
does each religion make?" You might want to give a few
examples of the type of claim each religion makes. You would
want to analyze these to see if there is anything distinctive

about the claims. Does one tradition make one type of claim
(maybe, moral claims), while another tradition focuses on a
different type (ritual claims, for example.) Another
possibility might be to analyze the same type of claim in all
three traditions; for example, you could isolate the claims
that each religion makes concerning the Absolute. Is there
something unique, for example, in the logic of the Jain claim
concerning the Absolute? If you choose this approach you
would be focusing on the structure of the claims, not on the
content of the claims.

The second part of the assignment asks you to step back
and examine what you have discovered in each religion. Are
the type of claims each religious tradition makes an
indication of a more general approach to truth? For example,
if a religion were to say that the Absolute could truthfully
be described in two, apparently contradictory, ways, what
would this show about that tradition's general theory of
truth? If a religious tradition thought that the Absolute
was totally beyond any linguistic assertions, what would this
show about that tradition's general theory of truth? To come
full circle, your conclusions concerning the theories of
truth embedded in the different traditions would, most
probably, form the basis for your overall thesis statement.

PART NINE   PROJECTS FOR DEVELOPING RELIGIOUS EMPATHY

1. One of the most distinctive teachings of India is the Jain
   reverence for life (ahimsa). The Jains believe that no
   living thing should be destroyed or harmed. Many
   individuals from other religious traditions respect the
   Jains for stressing the value of life and the idea of non-
   violence. Sometimes, however, these same people believe
   that the Jains take their beliefs to an extreme.

   You might try to practice for one day the Jain ideal of
   ahimsa. But this might turn out to be rather difficult.
   Rather, try to consider how you would have to live if you
   did practice ahimsa in this manner. Start by considering
   your clothing; what type of clothes could you wear if you
   did not want to harm any life? Would you have to walk
   around naked, as the Digambaras sect does? Could you wear
   wool or cotton clothes? What kind of shoes could you
   wear? Consider what type of food you could eat. Could

you eat meat or fish? Would eggs or diary produces by
acceptable? Could an argument be made against even
vegetables or grain? Finally, think about how we move
around. Would driving a car be allowed, since many
animals and insects are killed by cars? Would any form of
locomotion by acceptable? Could not even walking result
in stepping on ants or insects? In conclusion, you might
want to consider whether anybody could follow the path of
ahimsa a Western environment?

2. Many religions believe that there are actual evil beings
   or evil forces in the Universe. For the Zoroastrians, of
   course, this evil being was called Angra Mainyu. Other
   traditions might call the evil being Satan, or the Devil.
   Zoroastrianism is unique, however, in that it sees the
   struggle between good and evil being very much in doubt.
   Man must participate in this struggle, in order to aid the
   force of good.

   Read the newspaper for the day, and find one example of
   what you would consider "evil." This might be a war being
   fought in one part of the world, or it could be an awful
   crime that seems to have no reason behind it. How would
   your reaction to this event be different if you saw it as
   a struggle between equally powerful good and evil forces?
   Would evil make more sense if it was attributed to such an
   evil force? Would you feel less hope if you were not sure
   that the good force would win in the end?

ANSWER KEY TO SELF-TEST

B) Multiple Choice

1. d   6. a
2. b   7. a
3. b   8. a
4. b   9. c
5. d   10. d

C) True-False

1. T   6. F
2. T   7. T

3. F	8. T
4. F	9. T
5. T	10. F

Notes

[1]Selection from "Zendavesta," The Portable World Bible, ed. Robert O. Ballou (1944; New York: Penguin Books, 1985) 190-191.

[2]The Sikh Religion; Its Gurus, Sacred Writings and Anthems, ed. M. A. MacAuliffe, vol. 1 (Oxford: Clarendon Press, 1909) 35.

[3]Sri Umasvati Acarya, Tattvarthadhigama Sutra, in A Sourcebook in Indian Philosophy, ed. Sarvepalli Radhakrishnan et al., trans. J. L. Jaini (Princeton, N.J.: Princeton University Press, 1957) 252-253.

Chapter 6

RELIGIONS OF CHINA AND JAPAN

PART ONE   LEARNING OBJECTIVES

Doing these exercises, in conjunction with reading the
textbook, should help you to achieve the following
objectives. Read them and see how many you already have
mastered; then study the following terms and concepts, and
work through the exercises. After you have completed all the
exercises, return to this section and review the objectives
again.

You should be able to:

1. Describe the native Chinese beliefs, rituals and texts
   that formed the background to the thought of Confucius and
   Lao Tzu.

2. Explain what historical evidence regarding the lives of

Lao Tzu and Chuang Tzu, the date and authorship of the <u>Tao Te Ching</u> and the early historical development of Taoist philosophy.

3. Delineate and analyze in both discussion and writing the thought of the <u>Tao Te Ching</u>, and, in particular, its view of the Tao, human nature, the nature and role of the Sage, the relation of the individual to nature, and the relation of the individual to society.

4. Explain what is meant by magical Taoism, and what is meant by sectarian Taoism, and how these movements compare with the type of Taoism seen in the <u>Tao Te Ching</u> and the <u>Chuang Tzu</u>.

5. Name and describe at least two Taoist contemplation techniques, and show how these illustrate Taoist meditation.

6. Describe the historical situation during the latter Chou dynasty and relate this situation to the life of Confucius.

7. Delineate and analyze in both discussion and writing the thought of Confucius, and, in particular, his views concerning human nature, the nature and role of the <u>chun-tzu</u>, propriety (<u>li</u>) and benevolence (<u>jen</u>), and the relation of the individual to society.

8. Name at least two native Chinese schools of thought, besides the Taoists, who challenged Confucius's outlook, and give a brief description of the basic positions of each school.

9. Describe the basic course of development of Confucianism after Confucius, and give a brief description of the positions of at least three Confucian thinkers.

10. Discuss and write about the Taoist and Confucian Worldview, in particular, contrasting and comparing their views of the Absolute, the universe, the human role in the universe, the fundamental problem and resolution for human beings, community and ethics, and rituals and symbols.

11. Show the importance of education in the Confucian Worldview, and illustrate how this aspect of Confucianism

may have a continued influence in China and in other East
Asian societies.

12. Discuss the native Japanese view of man, nature and kami,
    and illustrate how aspects of this view is manifested in
    at least two myths preserved in the Kojiki, in ritual and
    in history.

13. Describe the basic course of development of Shinto from
    the time of Prince Shôtoku Taishi up through the Second
    World War. In particular, describe the changing
    relationship between Shinto and Buddhism.

14. Define and give illustrations of State Shinto, Shrine
    Shinto and Sectarian Shinto, including a discussion of the
    three major classifications of Sectarian Shinto.

15. Discuss and write about the Shinto Worldview, in
    particular, the Shinto view of the Absolute, the universe,
    the human role in the universe, the fundamental problem
    and resolution for human beings, community and ethics,
    rituals and symbols, and Shinto's relationship with other
    religions.

16. Analyze and write about the role of patriotism in Shinto
    and Japanese history, and the challenges in this area to
    contemporary Shinto.

PART TWO   TERMS AND INDIVIDUALS

                   A) CHINA

a) Terms and Concepts

Hsia dynasty	Shang dynasty
Chou dynasty	Son of Heaven
Tao	Yang
Yin	Heaven
Earth	wu-wei
Shang Ti	the Jade Emperor (Yu Huang)
Ling Pao	Tsao Shen
Three Purities	embryonic breathing (t'ai hsi)
shou-i	chun-tzu
li	yi

chung yung (the mean)   jen
shu   t'ien ming (Mandate of Heaven)
Mohist School   Fa-Chia School (Legalists)
Han dynasty   Neo-Confucianism
chi   tai chi
shih   ju

b) Individuals

Lao Tzu   Chuang Tzu
Ko Hung   Confucius (Kung-Fu-Tzu)
Mo Tzu   Kuan Chung
Han Fei Tzu   Mencius
Hsun Tzu   Chu Hsi
Sun Yat-sen   Chiang K'ai Shek
Mao Tse-tung

c) Texts

I Ching   Tao Te Ching
Pao P'u-tzu   Li Chi
Five Classics   Shu Ching
Shi Ching   Ch'un Ch'iu
Four Books   Analects (of Confucius)
The Great Learning   The Doctrine of the Mean
The Book of Mencius

d) Individuals and Terms from Other Traditions

Heraclitus   Niccolo Macheavelli
Aristotle   Buddha
Thomas Aquinas

B) JAPAN

a) Terms and Concepts

Shinto (kami no michi)   torii
kami   shaman
miko   Izanagi
Izanami   Yomi
Amaterasu   Susanoo
Tsukiyomi   Okunushi
Ninigi   bushido

harakiri (seppaku)
state Shinto
Ise Shrine
Shinto Taikyô
Shinto Shuseiha
Shinshukyô
Shinrikyô
Fusokyô
Jikkokyô
konjin
Misogikyô
Omoto
P. L. Kyodan
norito

shôgun
sectarian Shinto
kami-dana
Okuninushi no Kami
Shinto Taiseikyô
Honchi Taishin
Ontakekyô
Sengen Daishin
Kurozumikyô
Konkokyô
misogi harai
Tenri-kyô/Honmichi
Seicho-no-le
yamabushi

b) Individuals

Emperor Jimmu (legendary)
Emperor Shômu
Toyotomi Hideyoshi
Emperor Shôwa (Hirohito)
Kurozumi Munetada
Inoue Masakane
Onisaburo
Miki Tokuchika

Prince Shôtoku Taishi
Oda Nobunaga
Emperor Meiji
Yoshimura Masamochi
Kawate Bunjiro (Konko Daijin)
Deguchi Nao
Miki Nakayama
Taniguchi Masaharu

c) Texts

Kojiki

Nihongi

d) Individuals and Terms from Other Traditions

Commodore Matthew C. Perry
Zen Buddhism

Kokubun-ji temples

PART THREE   GUIDED REVIEW

1. Among the major religions studied in this chapter
_____ and _____ were originally Chinese, while
_____ is distinctively Japanese.

2. The earliest Chinese dynasty for which there is historical evidence is the _____ dynasty, whose dates were from _____ to _____.

3. The dynasty during which Confucius lived was the _____ dynasty, whose dates were from _____ to _____.

4. The Chinese believe that two forces are at work in the universe. The light and active force is termed _____. The dark and passive force is termed _____.

5. These two balancing forces are often correlated with another pair of terms: _____ and _____.

6. The _____ is an ancient text which uses sixty-four hexagrams and has been used for thousands of years by the Chinese for guidance and divination.

7. The beginnings of Taoism is usually ascribed to the possibly legendary figure, _____, who is credited with writing the text called the _____.

8. Taoists tend to emphasize not society, but _____. They argue that the best course to follow to achieve harmony is the _____ course.

9. For Lao Tzu "the door of all subtleties", that which a person should be in harmony with, is termed the _____.

10. The Taoists argue that one should act without acting. This Taoist concept is that of _____. An example a Taoist might give of this principle is _____.

11. The second major Taoist thinker was _____.

12. Magical Taoism was another form of Taoism that developed in China; it devoted its attention to such activities as _____ and _____.

13. The form of Taoism which developed temples and attempted to compete organizationally with Buddhism is termed _____.

14. For Taoism the best lifestyle is one that is _____ and _____.

15. One Greek thinker who had ideas similar to Taoism was
_____, who held that _____
_____.

16. One criticism that a Confucian might level against the
Taoist would be that _____
_____.

17. "Embryonic breathing", or t'ai-hsi, is _____
_____.

18. Confucius did not claim to present innovative ideas, but
rather claimed to present ideas that he believed were from
_____.

19. The condition of China during Confucius's lifetime can be
described as one of _____
_____.

20. During his lifetime Confucius travelled throughout China
in search of _____.

21. Confucius believed that humans were basically _____.

22. Confucius said that the _____ understood what
was moral and was at ease without being arrogant. However,
the _____ understood what was profitable and was
arrogant without being at ease.

23. The way things should be done, or appropriateness, is
termed in Chinese _____. When these rules become
internalized these are called _____.

24. Jen could be defined as _____.

25. Mo-tzu's central teaching was that _____
_____.

26. Whereas Confucius believed people should _____
their enemies, Mo-tzu responded that people should
_____ their enemies.

27. Han Fei Tzu was a member of the _____
School. This school argued that human nature was
_____.

28. One difference between Han Fei Tzu and Confucius was that Han Fei believed that the good ruler should govern through _____,   but Confucius believed the good ruler should govern through _____.

29. The Five Classics of Confucianism are:
_____,   _____,
_____, _____,   and
_____.   To these are added the Four Books:
_____, _____,
_____,   and _____.

30. Two influential later Confucianists were Mencius and Hsun Tzu. They differed in their assessment of human nature. Mencius viewed man's nature as basically _____, whereas Hsun Tzu thought man by nature was basically _____.

31. The great Neo-Confucian thinker Chu Hsi concluded that everything comes into being through _____ and _____.

32. Chu Hsi saw _____ as the ultimate principle in the Universe which is behind heaven and earth, behind yin and yang.

33. The Maoist view of Confucianism was that it
_____
_____.

34. The doctrine that the ruler's authority was derived from heaven, and that he could only continue to receive this authority as long as he cared for the welfare of the people and the state was termed _____.

35. Confucian ethics is based on reciprocity which means
_____.

36. The textbook focuses on one area in Chinese society where Confucius and Confucianism had a significant impact; this was _____.

37. Stunning natural phenomena, extraordinary people or objects, great leaders are all viewed in Shinto as _____.

38. According to Japanese myth, the islands of Japan were created by _____ .

39. In one of the most famous Japanese myths, Susanoo coaxed Amaterasu out of the cave by showing her a _____ .

40. According to many Japanese the kami and the Buddhist bodhisattvas and Buddhas are the _____ .

41. The code of Bushido reflects elements of _____ , _____ and _____ .

42. That form of Shinto which stressed the divine origin of Japan, the divinity of the Emperor and the duties of the individual to his country is _____ .

43. The center for observing reverence for the ancestors in a Japanese house is the _____ .

44. According to the Japanese Agency for Cultural Affairs, sectarian Shinto can be classified into three groups:
1) _____ ,
2) _____ , and
3) _____ .

45. Miki Nakayama founded the New Religion group termed _____ . It's Teaching of the Heavenly Reason is the belief that _____ .

46. In Shinto the deity who has been most venerated is _____ .

47. The Grand Ise Shrine was often the destination for _____ .

48. If one visited a Shinto shrine a visitor might typically see a Japanese do the following: _____ , _____ , _____ .

49. The author of the textbook claims that one of the issues facing Shinto today is whether it can help _____ _____ .

50. Japanese religion, the textbook states, is not so much a religion of _____, but rather is a religion of _____.

PART FOUR   ANALYZING TEXTS

Below are three texts that were not in the textbook. The texts, however, do contain ideas and concepts with which you should be familiar after reading the textbook. Read each text carefully, and try to analyze each by answering the following questions: What are the main ideas in the text? What viewpoint or viewpoints might the author of the text represent? Is it possible to identify the specific thinker, discipline, movement, tradition or work from which the text derives? What intellectual, literary, social, cultural or historical influences are reflected in the text? For each of your conclusions, try to point to specific evidence in the text (e.g. terms, ideas, arguments, writing style, etc.) which supports your conclusion. Be careful that your conclusions do not exceed the evidence upon which they rest.

TEXT ONE

The Master said, "I have transmitted what was taught to me without making up anything of my own. I have been faithful to and loved the Ancients. . . . I have listened in silence and noted what was said, I have never grown tired of learning nor wearied of teaching others what I have learned. . . . The thought that 'I have left my moral order untended, my learning unperfected, that I have heard of righteous men, but have been unable to go to them; have heard of evil men, but have been unable to reform them' - it is these thoughts that disquiet me."[1]

TEXT TWO

The True Way is one and the same, in every country and

throughout heaven and earth. This Way, however, has
been correctly transmitted only in our Imperial Land.
Its transmission in all foreign countries was lost long
ago in early antiquity, and many and varied ways have
been expounded, each country representing its own way as
the Right Way. . . . Let me state briefly what the one
original Way is. One must understand, first of all, the
universal principle of the world. The principle is that
Heaven and earth, all the gods and all phenomena, were
brought into existence by the creative spirits of two
deities - Takami-musubi and Kami-musubi. The birth of
all humankind in all ages and the existence of all
things and all matter have been the result of that
creative spirit. . . . This spirit of creativity is a
miraculously divine act the reason for which is beyond
the comprehension of the human intellect. [2]

TEXT THREE

Exterminate the sage, discard the wise
And the people will benefit a hundredfold;
Exterminate benevolence, discard rectitude,
And the people will again be filial;
Exterminate ingenuity, discard profit,
And there will be no more thieves and bandits.
These three, being false adornments, are not enough
And the people must have something to which they
            can attach themselves:
Exhibit the unadorned and embrace the uncarved block,
Have little thought of self and as few desires as
            possible. [3]

PART FIVE   SELF-TEST

a) Definitions and Descriptions - Write your own definition or
description of each of the following terms, individuals or
texts. After completing the self-test, check your answer
with the definition or description given in the textbook.

1. li _____
_____
_____.

2. wu wei _____
_____
_____.

3. torii _____
_____
_____.

4. yin _____
_____
_____.

5. bushido _____
_____
_____.

6. jen _____
_____
_____.

7. sectarian Shinto _____
_____
_____.

8. shou-i _____
_____
_____.

9. kami _____
_____
_____.

10.chung tzu _____
_____
_____.

b) Multiple Choice

1. Japanese emperors claimed to be descended from the Sun
   Goddess who was

a. Susanoo.
b. Tsukiyomi.
c. Izanagi.
d. Amaterasu.

2. The Confucian thinker who argued that man's nature is basically evil is

a. Mencius.
b. Confucius.
c. Hsun Tzu.
d. Chu Hsi.

3. The doctrine that the ruler gets his mandate to rule from heaven and that it is provisional on his governing the state on the basis of benevolence is called

a. Jen.
b. T'ien ming.
c. Chung yung.
d. T'ien.

4. Which of the following would best describe the beliefs of Lao Tzu?

a. The sage should love all people equally.
b. The sage should try to subdue and regulate nature.
c. The sage should seek harmony with the Tao.
d. The sage should seek to always be in accord with li.

5. Which dynasty did Confucius look to for guidance in how to order society and run a government?

a. Chou dynasty.
b. Shang dynasty.
c. Hsia dynasty.
d. Han dynasty.

6. Which the following practices is not mentioned as one of the practices of magical Taoism?

a. embryonic breathing
b. study of The Great Learning
c. alchemy
d. fortune-telling

7. Which of the following would be considered by the Japanese people as a kami?

    a. A famous leader from Japanese history.
    b. A majestic mountain.
    c. An large, old tree.
    d. All of the above.

8. The beginnings of Taoism are usually attributed to

    a. Lao Tzu
    b. Chuang Tzu
    c. Han Fei Tzu
    d. Mo Tzu

9. Which of the following is not one of the Five Relations of Confucianism?

    a. Elder brother-younger brother.
    b. Father-son.
    c. Ruler-subject.
    d. Mother-daughter.

10. Which of the following is not used by the Agency for Cultural Affairs as a classification for sectarian Shinto groups?

    a. Traditional sects.
    b. Mountain worship sects.
    c. Nichiren sects.
    d. Sects based on revelation.

C. True-False

T   F   1. For Chinese people, the Yang and the Yin are seen as balancing each other in the Tao.

T   F   2. In the famous Shinto myth, Izanami hid in a cave, and had to be lured out by Susanoo.

T   F   3. A Confucian scholar would act by following the principle of wu-wei.

T   F   4. The Legalist School believed that the ruler should govern his state through severe punishments.

T   F   5. In traditional Chinese thought, Yang is believed to be the passive, female, dark force in the universe.

T   F   6. Mencius was more concerned with the individual than was Confucius.

T   F   7. The earliest dynasty for which there is evidence is the Hsia dynasty.

T   F   8. State Shinto went through a period of rapid growth following Japan's surrender in 1945.

T   F   9. Lao Tzu was elevated to the status of a god in sectarian Taoism.

T   F   10. The main activity of the Fusokyô sect is climbing Mt. Fuji.

PART SIX   ESSAY AND DISCUSSION QUESTIONS

1. Analyze and compare the Indian worldview, as exemplified by Hinduism and Buddhism, and the Chinese worldview, as exemplified by Taoism and Confucianism.

2. What advice do you think Lao Tzu would give to a ruler? Do you think Lao Tzu's philosophy could be used to govern a country? Why or why not?

3. Confucius is held to have said:

   At 15, I had my mind bent on learning.
   At 30, I stood firm.
   At 40, I had no doubts.
   At 50, I knew the decrees of Heaven.
   At 60, my ear was an obedient organ for the reception of
          truth.
   At 70, I could follow what my heart desired, without
          transgressing what was right.

   How does the progression outlined in this quote illustrate Confucius's view of the Superior Man, and how one progresses towards this goal? Would Lao Tzu agree or disagree with this view of the Superior Man, and why?

4. Do you think Confucianism, as it is contained in the writings of Confucius and Mencius, is a religion? What would be your definition of religion?

5. Some scholars have argued that in Shinto the notion of "pollution" is important, but not the notion of "evil". Using evidence from Japanese myths and Shinto rituals and practices, evaluate the soundness of this statement. What do you think is the difference between the notion of "evil", and that of "pollution".

6. Describe the different types of Shinto, and discuss how they differ amongst themselves.

PART SEVEN   CONFRONTING QUESTIONS AND ISSUES

A) CHINA

In the spring of 1989 a movement for political reform and greater democracy began to spread in the People's Republic of China. It spread first among Chinese university students, and then among Chinese workers, and peasants. At the center of this movement was a large group of Chinese young people who encamped in Beijing's Tian'anmen Square, the symbolic center of the Socialist state. After appearing to tolerate the growth and spread of the movement, the Chinese leadership finally ordered army troops and tanks to clear the square. In one day, June 4, the troops killed hundreds of the people in or near the square. Thousands of the leaders and members of the democracy movement were hunted down, and put on trial. Some were executed. Many more were sent to prison.

The textbook asks, "How much Confucian influence remains among the Chinese people?" Using the events in the Spring of 1989 as a test case, to what extent can one make a connection between the ancient teachings of China - Confucianism, Taoism and Legalism - and the contemporary political situation? What are the similarities, if any, between the students' ideals of reforming a corrupt political system and achieving

greater democracy, and the ideals of the traditional systems?
Would any of the teachings be supportive of democracy?
Which, if any, of the schools of thought would have counseled
the Chinese government to act as it did? Which, if any, of
the schools of thought would have counseled against such a
course of action? Finally, does your analysis indicate that
the ancient teachings still resonate in modern China, or that
they have little relevancy when discussing today's China?

B) JAPAN

World events in the closing years of the Twentieth
Century hold promise for a new world order, a new
internationalism. The integration of the European market,
the increasingly international nature of finance and
business, the linking of world communications through
satellites and computer networks, and the ending of the Cold
War are all factors promoting this new order. Today, a
nation and a people who define themselves in terms of a
consciousness of nationalism (in Japanese, kokuminshigi)
appear to run the danger of being excluded from the new
international community.

It is not surprising, therefore, that one of the major
topics of debate in Japan is how, and to what degree, Japan
should become more "international". Implicit within this
debate is a tension that the Japanese confront between a
strong sense of their national uniqueness and a desire to
build on what they share with other peoples. As the textbook
states, "[Shinto] is so much a part of the ethnic life of
Japanese people that it must be included wherever their
cultural identity is considered." Given your study of the
beliefs and rituals of Shinto, what role, if any, can Shinto
play in the Japanese search for a new international role? Is
Shinto a belief system that can only lead the Japanese to an
awareness of their national uniqueness? Are their elements
within Shinto that can help the Japanese to define a new
international consciousness? What might be these elements,
if they exist?

PART EIGHT   AN ESSAY FOR DEEPER CONSIDERATION

Essay Question

You are the Emperor of China. A group of dedicated political activists have barricaded themselves, along with a number of hostages, in a house in the capital. The group claims that you, the Emperor, have failed to fulfill the Mandate of Heaven (t'ien ming), and, therefore, demands that you resign. Failure to comply with this demand, the group states, might result in harm to the hostages and destruction of the entire neighborhood.

You call a crisis meeting of your chief ministers. Among these advisors are Confucius, Lao Tzu and Han Fei Tzu. You tell each advisor that you want him to address the following questions: Who constitutes the Good Ruler? What is the criteria or standard the Good Ruler should use when making decisions? Finally, how can this standard be used to make a decision in this crisis? You will listen in turn to each minister's answers, and then decide which course of action to pursue.

Write an essay in which you indicate what answers each of the three advisors would give to the Emperor, and which position you, the Emperor, would adopted, and why.

Tips For Answering

This is a very complex essay question. In order to answer the question well it requires the student to address a number of different problems. Perhaps one of the most important points to notice about this essay question is what it is not asking. It is not really asking you to decide what course of action each thinker would recommend in this crisis. Or rather, it is interested in using this simple question to raise a group of more sophisticated questions. It is these more complex questions that you are being asked to address. What are these questions?

The first of these questions is "Who is a Good Ruler?" What are the qualities or characteristics that define a leader or a ruler as being good or wise? Each of the three thinkers addresses this question in the works attributed to them. The answers they propose may agree on some points, but ultimately each thinker gives a very different description of the best type of ruler. What are the positions of each advisor and how do they differ?

What makes a ruler good or wise, it could be argued, is that he is able to act properly, and make the correct decisions for the good of his state. But this raises another question, what standard or criteria should a ruler employ in order to decide how to act? Is a good ruler one who preserves order in his country? Or is he one who the people respect and love? Or could it be that the good ruler is one who insures his own continued rule? Arriving at an answer to this question may in fact be necessary before one can define the Good Ruler.

There may be one more question even more deeply embedded in the essay assignment. It could be argued that for each of these Chinese thinkers their positions on the criteria that define good government are driven by their views on the nature of humans. Is man basically good or evil? Is it possible to make man better through education or religious practice, or will man always be untrustworthy? The answers that each thinker gave to these questions helped to determine what role, if any, he saw for government. In your essay, you might want to begin by examining each thinker's views on the nature of man.

Once you have addressed these questions in your essay it may be possible to say what specific advice each of these ancient Chinese thinkers might have given to the Emperor. Given the nature of man, and therefore the nature of good government, what specific action would be appropriate in this situation? And with which view of man, of government and of this crisis do you, the Emperor, agree? This is the decision that you need to make, but be sure to indicate what factors and reasons support your conclusions.

PART NINE   PROJECTS FOR DEVELOPING RELIGIONS EMPATHY

1. The Heart of the Dragon is an excellent documentary series
   on modern China produced by the British Broadcasting
   Corporation and shown a number of years ago on the Public
   Broadcasting Service here in America. Each episode of the

series focuses on one aspect of Chinese culture, for
example, marriage and the familty, or the justice system.
Two of the hour-long episodes deal specifically with
various aspects of China's traditional teachings. If your
college owns copies of this video you might want to see if
you could borrow or arrange to view these episodes. You
might also be able to find this video at a rental store
that specializes in foreign and art videos.

The segment called "Knowing" examines ancient Chinese
science and technology, and its relation to China's recent
attempts to modernize. Among the issues discussed is the
role of Taoism and other alchemical and magical practices
in ancient Chinese science. As you view this segment you
might want to consider how ancient Chinese science was
different from or similar to the science you might be
studying at school. Would a scientist of today, do you
think, accept what was being done as true "science"? Why?
Also, you could consider what role Taoism and such ideas
as yin-yang played in Chinese science? Is Taoism
functioning here as a religion? As a science? As a
philosophy? As a psuedo-science? If you would like to
read more about science in ancient China, a work of truly
impressive scholarship is Joseph Needham's multi-volume
Science and Civilization in China.

The other episode that deals with the religious traditions
of China is the one titled "Believing". A portion of the
episode examines the beliefs of modern China, and, in
particular, the Chinese belief (or lack of belief) in what
one of the speakers terms "Marxist-Leninist-Mao Tse-Tung
Socialist Thought". The central part of the hour,
however, examines the traditional belief systems of China:
folk religion, Buddhism, Taoism and Confucianism. This
program raises a number of provocative issues you might
want to consider. First, it makes the claim that much of
the moral and social education shown in this episode is as
Confucian as it is Maoist or Socialist. Is this true?
Second, it claims that Confucianism should not be
considered a religion, but rather a code of social
behavior. Is this true? Can you figure out what
definition of "religion" the program employs when it makes
this judgement? Watch the program, examine some examples
of how the Chinese live, and see if you agree with the
conclusions of the program.

2. You might consider visiting a martial arts center or dôjô
   by yourself, or with a friend from the class. Many of the
   martial arts developed in China, Japan and Korea, and were
   influenced by various aspects of Confucianism, Taoism and
   Buddhism. You might be especially interested in observing
   the ancient Chinese practice of Tai Chi Chuan, which
   exhibits many of the ideas discussed in Taoism.

   If there is an instructor of Tai Chi in your area, ask him
   or her if you might visit a class and observe the students
   practicing their art. Explain that you are studying
   Chinese religion, and would be interested in seeing how
   some of these ideas may have influenced the martial arts.
   If you have this opportunity, pay attention to the nature
   of Tai Chi. What role does "balance" play in Tai Chi? Do
   you see any influences from the traditional teachings of
   China? Does the "form", the dance-like movement that is
   practiced everyday, connect to any of the ideas or
   practices you have studied? Also observe, if you can, the
   more advanced students practicing "push-hands". What is
   the goal of such a practice? Would any of the Chinese
   thinkers be interested in such a practice? Why?

3. There are few gardens in the world as beautiful or serene
   as the best gardens of Japan. There are also few places
   where one can better observe the spirit of Shinto than in
   a Japanese style garden. The Japanese style garden has
   been influenced by many traditions over the centuries.
   Depending on the type and period of the Japanese garden,
   Zen or Pure Land Buddhism may have been very influential.
   However, Shinto has affected almost all styles of Japanese
   gardens. The very notion of setting aside an area for a
   garden is akin to the Shinto practice of marking off a
   Shinto shrine or a special tree or rock as the location of
   the kami.

   Many places in America now have a Japanese style garden
   that is open to the public. There are in Philadelphia,
   where this is being written, presently at least three
   Japanese gardens one can visit. If you have such a garden
   in your area, set aside some time for a visit. During
   your visit, first just observe the garden, and enjoy the
   views. Try to feel the mood that the garden creates.
   After a time, analyze more closely the specific elements
   that were combined to make the garden. What aspects of
   the garden seem different from a more Western style

garden? Can you pick out any elements in the garden that may reflect a Shinto influence? What roles do rocks, trees and water play in the garden? Are any of these elements set aside in a special manner? If there are any buildings or man-made artifacts in the garden, what is their relation to the natural elements? Do they seem to contrast with the natural elements or harmonize with them? What type of order, if any, does the garden seem to project?

Those who can not visit a Japanese garden in person may want to learn about them by reading and examining pictures. Teiji Itoh has written a number of excellent books on the Japanese garden. Much the same questions can be asked as you look at the pictures in a good book on Japanese gardens.[4] But no book can ever substitute for the enjoyment of a visit to a peaceful garden on a beautiful Spring afternoon.

ANSWER KEY TO SELF-TEST SECTION

b) Multiple Choice

1. d	6. b
2. c	7. d
3. b	8. a
4. c	9. d
5. a	10. c

c) True-False

1. T	6. T
2. F	7. F
3. F	8. F
4. T	9. T
5. F	10. T

Notes

[1]Confucius, The Analects of Confucius, VII: 1-3, trans. Arthur Waley (New York: Vintage Books, 1938) 123

[2]Motoori Norinaga, Motoori Norinaga Zenshû, VI: 3-6, in Sources of Japanese Tradition, ed. Ryusaku Tsunoda et al., (New York: Columbia University Press, 1958) 520-521.

[3]Lao Tzu, Tao To Ching, XIX, trans. D. C. Lau (New York: Penguin Books, 1963) 75.

[4]Teiji Itoh, The Japanese Garden, New Haven: Yale Press, 1972.

Teiji Itoh, Space and Illusion in the Japanese Garden, New York: Weatherhill/Tankosha, 1973.

Chapter 7

JUDAISM

PART ONE   LEARNING OBJECTIVES

Doing these exercises, in conjunction with reading the textbook, should help you to achieve the following objectives. Read them and see how many you already have mastered; then study the following terms and concepts, and work through the exercises. After you have completed all the exercises, return to this section and review the objectives again.

You should be able to:

1. Analyze the nature of Torah and discuss its significance and role in Judaism.

2. Examine the concept of a "revealed-historical religion", how Judaism is a revealed-historical religion, and how this contrasts with the religions studied earlier.

3. Outline the stories of Abraham's covenant with God, and the Exodus from Egypt, and analyze the importance of "covenant" in the history of the Jewish people.

4. Describe the nature and characteristics of the Prophetic Movement, including at least two pre-exilic prophets and their messages.

5. Explain how modern scholarship believes the Pentateuch was edited, and the significance of these discoveries.

6. Analyze the development of Judaism from the post-exilic prophets to the beginning of the Roman administration of Palestine, including a discussion of the beginning of synagogue worship, the Greek influence on Judaism, and the nature of Wisdom literature.

7. Describe Judaism during the Roman administration of Palestine, including the Messianic movements, Jewish revolts against Roman rule and the birth of Rabbinic Judaism.

8. Define what is meant by Talmudic Judaism, explain the process by which the Talmud was compiled and discuss the centrality of Talmud for Jewish life.

9. Offer an overall description of Medieval Judaism, illustrating this by reference to at least two Medieval philosophers and Medieval Jewish mysticism.

10. Describe the changes Judaism went through during the Modern Age, including the influence of the Enlightenment on Jewish thinkers and the birth of the Reform, Conservative and Reconstructionist movements.

11. Recognize and discuss the importance of the Holocaust and the State of Israel for Judaism in the Twentieth Century.

12. Discuss and write about the Worldview of Judaism, in particular, the views of Judaism on the Absolute, the universe, the human role in the universe, the fundamental problem and resolution for human beings, community and ethics, symbols and rituals, and life after death.

13. Examine alternative definitions of the concept of "chosen people", and what role this idea has played in the Jewish

understanding.

14. Explain the concept of <u>kashruth</u>, and discuss how diet and food can be an expression of a religious commitment.

PART TWO   TERMS AND INDIVIDUALS

A) Terms and Concepts

monotheism	Western Wall (Wailing Wall)
Temple Mount	Jerusalem
Mesopotamia	Judaism
covenant	sacrifice
Passover	matzah
Mount Sinai	Ark of the Covenant
theocracy	Shema
"Ehyeh-Asher-Ehyeh"	Wellhausen school
Canaan	Canaanites
Baal	Asherah
seer	Levites
Hebrews	Samaria
prophets	Assyrians
the First Temple	Babylonian Exile
Yahweh	Elohim
"J"	"E"
"D"	"P"
synagogue	rabbi
Judea	scribe
Seleucids of Syria	Hellenism
Sabbath	circumcision
Maccabean revolt	Hanukkah
Romans	Saducees
Zealots	Essenes
Pharisees	Qumran community
Platonism	allegorical method
the Second Temple	Masada
Messiah (Annointed of God)	kosher
"king's serfs"	Karaites
Geonim	Kabbalah
En Soph	ghetto
the Inquisition	mensch
Reform Judaism	Pittsburgh Platform

Orthodox Judaism	Conservative Judaism
Columbus Platform	Zionism
mitzvot	kashrut
kosher	yamulkes
Reconstructionism	Hasidism
Zaddik	Balfour Declaration
Holocaust	kibbutzim
Adonai	sheol
halakhah	aggadah
written law	oral law
shofar	Rosh Hashana
Yom Kippur	Hanukkah
Purim	Passover
Shavuot	Haggadah
Seder	Bar Mitzvah
Bat Mitzvah	huppah
shohet	Sanhedrin

B) <u>Individuals</u>

King Solomon	Abraham
Sarah	Lot
Isaac	Ishmael
Jacob (Israel)	Joseph
Moses	Joshua
Samuel	Saul
David	Solomon
Rehoboam	Elijah
Queen Jezebel	Bathsheba
Nathan	Amos
Hosea	Isaiah
Micah	Nebuchadnezzar
Ezra	Ezekiel
Jeremiah	Second Isaiah (Deutro-Isaiah)
Nehemiah	Antiochus IV
Mattathias	Judas (son of Mattathias)
Pompey	Judas the Galilean
Pilate	Philo Judaeus
Florus	Vespasian
Titus	Flavius Josephus
Flavius Silva	Yohanan ben Zakkai
Rabbi Akiba	Bar Kokhba
Hadrian	Rabbi Hillel
Rabbi Meir	Rabbi Judah
Saadia ben Joseph	Anan ben David
Judah Halevi	Moses ben Maimon (Maimonides)

Moses de Leon
King Ferdinand
Baruch Spinoza
Abraham Geiger
Samson Raphael Hirsch
Isaac Meyer Wise
Mordecai Kaplan
Elie Wiesel
Hermann Cohen
Chaim Weizmann
David Ben-Gurion
Leo Baeck

Isaac Luria
Queen Isabella
Moses Mendelssohn
Zacharias Frankel
David Einhorn
Solomon Schecter
Israel Baal Shem
Martin Buber
Captain Alfred Dreyfus
Anne Frank
Golda Meir
Herman Wouk

C) Texts

The Torah
The Jewish Bible (Tanakh)
Exodus
Numbers
The Prophets (Nevi'im)
Judges
First and Second Kings
Jeremiah
Hosea
Amos
Jonah
Nahum
Zephaniah
Zechariah
The Writings (Kethuvim)
Proverbs
Song of Songs
Lamentations
Esther
Ezra
First and Second Chronicles
Wisdom literature
Babylonian Talmud
Mishneh Torah
Guide for the Perplexed
Zohar
I and Thou
The Idea of the Holy
This is My God

Talmud
Genesis
Leviticus
Deuteronomy
Joshua
First and Second Samuel
Isaiah
Ezekiel
Joel
Obadiah
Micah
Habakkuk
Haggai
Malachi
Psalms
Job
Ruth
Ecclesiastes
Daniel
Nehemiah
Septuagint
Gemarah
The Kuzari
Shirei Ziyyon (Poems of Zion)
Yigdal
Nathan the Wise
The Jewish State
Judaism and Christianity

D) <u>Individuals and Terms From Other Traditions</u>

Christianity   Islam
muezzin   Muslim
Dome of the Rock   Muhammad
Isis   Horus
Marduk   Babylonians
cyrus of Persia   Alexander the Great
Aristotle   Clement
Origen   John Locke
Rene Descartes   Gotthold Ephraim Lessing
Rudolph Otto   John the Baptist
Jesus of Nazareth   King Herod

PART THREE   GUIDED REVIEW

1. Judaism is a _____ religion, which means
that it teaches belief in one God.

2. The three main headings of the Jewish Bible are _____
_____, _____ and _____.

3. One of the main acts of worship in Judaism from the time
of Abraham until the destruction of the Second Temple was
_____.

4. The idea of a covenant is a _____.

5. The Jewish holiday of Passover commemorates _____
_____.

6. The unleaven bread that is eaten during Passover
symbolizes _____.

7. The wooden chest containing the tablets with the Ten
Commandments was called _____.

8. The <u>Shema</u> is _____.

9. The religion of the Canaanites consisted of _____
_____.

10. Prophets in Judaism were those who _____
_____.

11. The image that Hosea used in his teachings was that of Israel as _____ .

12. When the First Temple was destroyed, most of the Jews who were living in Judah were exiled to _____ .

13. According to most Biblical scholars the first five books are edited documents that contain the writings of _____ sources.

14. Scholars label these writers as _____ , _____ , _____ and _____ . The work of Deuteronomy is credited to _____ .

15. The difference between the Temple and the synagogue worship was that worship in the Temple centered around _____ , while worship in the synagogue centered around _____ .

16. The rabbi differs from the priest in that he _____ _____ .

17. Scholars believe that chapters forty through sixty-six in the book of the Bible termed <u>Isaiah</u> were written by _____ _____ at the time of _____ _____ .

18. The influential Greek translation of Hebrew scriptures is the _____ .

19. Wisdom literature is _____ _____ .

20. The Maccabees were _____ . It was during their struggle that the events occurred that are the basis for the Jewish holiday of _____ .

21. During the time of Roman rule of Palestine the Jewish party that believed in a forceful overthrow of Roman rule was the _____ .

22. The Pharisees were _____ _____ .

23. The highest Jewish court and the governing Jewish body before the destruction of the Second Temple was

_____ .

24. The incident that sparked the Jewish rebellion against the Romans was _____.

25. The canon of the Jewish Bible was assembled by _____ C.E.

26. The Babylonian Talmud is a combination of the _____ and the _____. The nature of the Talmud is _____.

27. Saadia ben Joseph is famous for combining _____ _____.

28. The Thirteen Articles of Maimonides includes as essential beliefs of Judaism belief in the _____ and the _____ of God.

29. According to the Zohar the world that we experience through our senses is _____ _____. At the top of a hierarchy of male-female dualities is _____.

30. During the Medieval Period many Jews made a living by lending money because _____ and because _____.

31. Under Ferdinand and Isabella the Jews living in Spain had to choose between _____ and _____.

32. Spinoza was excommunicated by the rabbis because he taught such ideas as _____.

33. The teachings of Moses Mendelssohn took the position that people of different religions _____.

34. The three main branches of Judaism in the United States are _____, _____ and _____.

35. In regard to keeping Kosher, Reform Judaism _____ _____.

36. Mordecai Kaplan founded the school known as _____ _____.

37. The term Hasidim means _____.

38. Today, the term "The Holocaust" refers to _____
_____.

39. The cooperative farms that have played a major role in building the State of Israel are called _____.

40. Judaism has usually expressed the nature of God in the analogy of a _____.

41. Judaism's view of the nature of the world and the body is
_____.

42. Mitzvot could be defined as _____.

PART FOUR   ANALYZING TEXTS

Below are three texts that were not in the textbook. The texts, however, do contain ideas and concepts with which you should be familiar after reading the textbook. Read each text carefully, and try to analyze each by answering the following questions: What are the main ideas in the text?   What viewpoint or viewpoints might the author of the text represent? Is it possible to identify the specific thinker, discipline, movement, tradition or work from which the text derives? What intellectual, literary, social, cultural or historical influences are reflected in the text? For each of your conclusions, try to point to specific evidence in the text (e.g. terms, ideas, arguments, writing style, etc.) which supports your conclusion. Be careful that your conclusions do not exceed the evidence upon which they rest.

TEXT ONE

When she pursues her lovers she will not overtake them,
    when she looks for them she will not find them;
        then she will say,
'I will go back to my husband again;
    I was better off with him than I am now.'
For she does not know that it is I who gave her
    corn, new wine, and oil,
    I who lavished upon her silver and gold

which they spent on the Baal.
Therefore I will take her back
my corn at the harvest and my new wine at the vintage,
    and I will take away the wool and the flax
        which I gave her to cover her naked body;
    so I will show her up for the lewd thing she is . . .

I will punish her for the holy days
when she burnt sacrifices to the Baalim.[1]

TEXT TWO

MISHNAH.   Every kind of flesh is forbidden to be cooked
in milk, excepting the flesh of fish and of locusts;
and it is also forbidden to place upon the table [flesh]
with cheese, excepting the flesh of fish and of locusts.
If a person vowed to abstain from flesh, he may partake
of the flesh of fish and of locusts.

GEMARA.   It follows [from our Mishnah] that the flesh of
fowls is prohibited by the law of Torah; now in
accordance with whose view would this be? It surely is
not in accordance with R. Akiba's view, for R. Akiba
maintains that the flesh of wild animals and of fowls is
not prohibited by the law of Torah. Consider now the
final clause,"if a person vowed to abstain from flesh,
he may partake of the flesh of fish and locusts." It
follows however that he is forbidden the flesh of fowl,
which is in accordance with R. Akiba's view, namely,
that any variation concerning which the agent would ask
for special instructions is deemed to be of the same
species. . . R. Joseph said, The author [of our
Mishnah] is Rabbi [Judah the Prince] who incorporated
the views of various Tannaim: with regard to vows he
adopted the view of R. Akiba, and with regard to flesh
[cooked] in milk he adopted the view of the Rabbis.[2]

TEXT THREE

We recognize in the Bible the record of the consecration
of the Jewish people to its mission as the priest of the
one God, and value it as the most potent instrument of
religious and moral instruction. . . We recognize in the

Mosaic legislation a system of training the Jewish people for its mission during it national life in Palestine, and today we accept as binding only its moral laws, and maintain only such ceremonies as elevate and sanctify our lives, but reject all such as are not adapted to the view and habits of modern civilization. [3]

PART FIVE   SELF-TEST

A) Definitions and Descriptions - Write your own definition or description of each of the following terms, individuals or texts. After completing the self-test, check your answer with the definition or description given in the textbook.

1. mitzvot _____

_____

_____.

2. Haggadah _____

_____

_____.

3. Pharisees _____

_____

_____.

4. halakhah _____

_____

_____.

5. synagogue _____

_____

_____.

6. Shema _____

_____

_____.

7. "J" _____

_____

_____.

8. rabbi _____
_____
_____.

9. Passover _____
_____
_____.

10. Gemarah _____
_____
_____.

B) Multiple Choice

1. The branch of Judaism in America that attempts to moderate
between the rejection of all rituals and mitzvot, and a
very strict observation of all traditional obligations is

   a. Conservative Judaism.
   b. Orthodox Judaism.
   c. Reform Judaism.
   d. Reconstructionist Judaism.

2. Which of the following is not one of the three divisions
of the Hebrew Bible?

   a. Torah
   b. Wisdom
   c. Prophets
   d. Writings

3. The Greek translation of the Hebrew Bible was the

   a. Vulgate.
   b. Tanakh.
   c. Septuagint.
   d. Wisdom literature.

4. Which one of the following is not used to denote an author
of material in the first five books of the Bible?

   a. "J"
   b. "T"
   c. "P"
   d. "E"

5. The juristic tradition, or legal material from the Torah, is called

    a. Midrash
    b. Talmud
    c. Aggadah
    d. Halakhah

6. Which of the following was not one of the Jewish sects at the time of Jesus of Nazareth?

    a. Essenes
    b. Sanhedrin
    c. Zealots
    d. Sadducees

7. Which Jewish holiday commemorates the Exodus from Egypt?

    a. Yom Kippur
    b. Rosh Hashana
    c. Purim
    d. Passover

8. The teachers who called Israel back to a pure religion, and also criticized the reliance on sacrificial rites were called

    a. Priests.
    b. Rabbis
    c. Prophets.
    d. Sages.

9. It could be said that Judaism begins with whose encounter with God?

    a. Moses
    b. Joseph
    c. David
    d. Abraham

10. The Medieval Jewish thinker who formulated 13 articles that all Jews should agree upon was

    a. Moses Mendelssohn.
    b. Judah Halevi.

c. Maimonides.
d. Saadia ben Joseph.

C) <u>True-False</u>

T   F   1. Bar Kokhba was held to be the Messiah
               by the famous Rabbi Akiba.

T   F   2. Most scholars believe that the Torah
               was written by Moses.

T   F   3. The Babylonian Talmud is a combination of t
               the Misnah and the Gemarah.

T   F   4. <u>The Zohar</u> believed that this world is the
               highest reality.

T   F   5. Spinoza believed that the Old Testament
               taught an idea of immortality.

T   F   6. Reconstructionalism rejects any supernatural
               elements in Judaism.

T   F   7. The position of the Conservative Movement
               was set out in the Pittsburgh Platform.

T   F   8. Judaism could be classified as a revealed-
               historic religion.

T   F   9. A <u>scribe</u> was the person who wrote down the
               teachings of the prophets as the spoke.

T   F   10. The book called "Isaiah" contains the
               writings of at least two different prophets.

PART SIX   ESSAY AND DISCUSSION QUESTIONS

1. Examine the role of Torah in Jewish history. Would it be
   accurate to claim that Judaism is the way of Torah?

2. Explain how the first five books of the Jewish Bible were
   written and edited.

3. What does the term "covenant" mean, and how could the history of the Jewish people be understood as an ongoing covenant between God and his people?

4. Using two pre-exilic prophets, describe the Prophetic movement, and examine in what sense it was a challenge to the Temple centered religion?

5. What were some of the basic differences between the Judaism of the time of Jesus and the Second Temple, and the Rabbinic Judaism that evolved after the destruction of the temple?

6. What was the Talmud and what role did it play in Medieval Judaism? What does the author mean when he says "Medieval Judaism was Talmudic Judaism?"

6. What is distinctive about Jewish mysticism?

7. What role does Israel play in modern Judaism? What challenges face Israel in the future?

PART SEVEN   CONFRONTING ISSUES AND ANSWERS

    The author of the textbook mentions a number of issues that confront modern day Judaism. Near the top of any such list for almost all Jews in America is the question of Israel. American Jews have loyally and strongly supported Israel throughout her existence, and they continue to do so today. Given the horror of the Holocaust and the tenuous position of Jews in so much of the world, American Jews believe that the existence of the State of Israel is vital for all Jews. While almost all Jews support the existence of a Jewish state, however, this does not mean that there is not a debate over what should be the nature of such a state. For many Jews, Israel is not just a physical location or a political entity, it is also a symbol. The question for many Israelis, American Jews and friends of Israel is how to define the symbolic nature of Israel.

    Consider and reflect on some of the following questions: What does the establishment of the state of Israel mean in conjunction with the Holocaust? Does the existence of Israel

serve as a sign of hope in the face of such utter evil?
Should Israel be a model for other nations, and if so, does
this mean that Israel should be held to higher standards than
her neighbors? Can Israel afford to be held to higher
standards than other countries? Can she afford not to be
held to higher standards? Is Israel primarily a political
entity, or is it also a spiritual and a moral entity? If
Israel is primarily a Jewish state, what does that mean?
Does it mean that non-Jews in the country are not full
citizens? If you are Jewish, you have probably thought about
these questions a great deal. If you are not Jewish, you
might want to talk about them with a close Jewish friend.
Listen carefully to understand how your friend feels about
these issues, and how they influence his or her life.

PART EIGHT   AN ESSAY FOR DEEPER CONSIDERATION

Essay Question

   Ludwig Lewisohn raises the question in this manner: "What
is a Jew? What is it to be a Jew? Are Jews a religious
community, like the Roman or Greek Churches? Or are Jews an
ethnic group, like the Negroes? Or are they a secular
community, formed by historic forces, which is a vague enough
term, like the Danes or the Dutch?"[4] Another, less
existentialist, way of phrasing this query is, what is
normative Judaism? What are the criteria, if any, that
determine if an individual remains within the bounds of
Judaism?

   Examine this question in light of your study of Judaism.
Illustrate your points with specific references to the
thinkers, ideas or movements you have studied.

Tips For Answering

   One of the major points you should discuss in your essay
is the proposed answers that Lewisohn mentions in the quote.
He suggests three alternative answers: Judaism as a
religious community, as an ethnic group and as a secular
community. Using Lewisohn's alternatives you could approach
the problem in the following fashion:

a) You first could clarify the meaning of each of these terms. What does each of these terms mean? Are the examples he gives clarifying or confusing? Can you think of any other alternatives?

b) After you have clarified the three choices you could examine the evidence from Jewish history and belief. Does either of these three choices explain how Jews have identified themselves, and drawn the bounds of the community? Are the criteria for being Jewish religious, social or ethnic criteria?

c) If none of these three options explains what being Jewish means, could some combination of the three be more accurate? Lewisohn does not consider this alternative, and it may be the case that Judaism is a combination of the three aspects.

d) Your essay could also consider a more radical answer. Perhaps what makes one Jewish is something like a relationship to history, or a commitment to a covenant. Indeed, this is the general approach that Lewisohn takes later in his article. You should consider the possibility that Judaism functions in a unique way among world religions.

PART NINE   PROJECTS FOR DEVELOPING RELIGIOUS EMPATHY

1. Since the destruction of the Second Temple one of the centers of Judaism has been the synagogue. A synagogue is a place for prayer and a place to read and study Torah. Many synagogues welcome visits by a person trying to better understand Judaism.

   If you have a Jewish friend who belongs to a congregation ask if you might visit a service with him or her. You might want your friend to explain beforehand what will occur during the service, and what are the different aspects of the service. It might also be helpful and polite to meet the rabbi beforehand, and explain why you will be attending. He or she would probably be glad to answer any questions that you might have.

   During the Sabbath service observe the congregation, how are they acting? Do they seem to be focused on the rabbi, or are they interacting among themselves? What is the

inter-personal dynamic? How is the inside of the
synagogue structured? Where is the center of attention?
Does there seem to be a hierarchical arrangement of space?
Are any special items of clothing being worn by the people
and the rabbi, and if so, what do they signify? Is music
part of the ritual? If it is, how would you describe the
music? Are there any artistic representations inside the
synagogue? If so, where are they, and what is their
nature? How might what you see be different if you were
in a Reform (or Conservative, or Orthodox) congregation?
What does the Jewish ritual and worship you see here
indicate about the nature of Jewish faith and belief?

2. The horror of the Holocaust, during which at least six
   million Jews were killed, is an event that no one can
   fully understand, and yet an event people should never
   forget. A number of excellent documentary films have been
   made on the Holocaust, but one of the best is the black
   and white film Night and Fog. Many colleges have copies
   of the film, as do the better video stores. Try to get a
   copy and watch it. It is not a movie designed to make you
   feel good, but it will raise questions that can not be
   ignored.

   Among the questions you should ponder as you watch the
   film are: Where was God when such a thing happened?
   Could there be a God if there is so much evil in the
   world? Which was more evil, committing such acts, or not
   protesting the commission of such acts? What is the
   meaning of the Jews as a chosen people? Is the image that
   Second Isaiah uses of a suffering servant applicable here,
   or does this level of brutality render that concept
   meaningless, or worse? Is the message of the Holocaust
   that Jews must rely on themselves to survive, not trusting
   in other nations?

ANSWER KEY TO SELF-TEST

B) Multiple Choice

1. a   6. b
2. b   7. d
3. c   8. c
4. b   9. d
5. d   10. c

C) True-False

1. T   6. T
2. F   7. F
3. T   8. T
4. F   9. F
5. F   10. T

Notes

[1]Hosea II:7-13, <u>The New English Bible</u> (Oxford, Oxford University Press, 1970).

[2]<u>Mishnah</u> VIII.1, <u>Gemara</u> page 104a, <u>The Babylonian Talmud</u>, ed. I. Epstein, Part I, Vol.4 (London: The Soncino Press, 1948) 576.

[3]"The Pittsburgh Platform" Article 2, 3, <u>Basic Sources of the Judaeo-Christian Tradition</u>, Fred Berthold, et al. (Engelwood Cliffs, N.J.: Prentice-Hall, Inc., 1962) 350.

[4]Ludwig Lewisohn, <u>What is This Jewish Heritage?</u> (New York: Bnai Brith Hillel Foundations, 1954) 1.

Chapter 8

CHRISTIANITY

PART ONE   LEARNING OBJECTIVES

1. Relate the life story of Jesus of Nazareth, discussing how events in his life exemplifies Christian teachings and the significance for Christians of Jesus's life, death and resurrection.

2. Write about and analyze the teachings of Jesus as they are contained in the Gospel accounts, addressing the issue of how Jesus's teaching compared and contrasted with that of the Judaism of his day.

3. Explain why the significance of the Resurrection for Christians, and describe how Paul interpreted the meaning of the Resurrection and the Christian message.

4. Examine the issue of "Christology" (the study of who Jesus was and who his followers thought he was), exploring how

Jesus referred to himself and saw himself, and how the early Jesus movement and the early Church attempted to understand Jesus's nature and role.

5. Discuss the development of the early Church, including how the Church addressed the question of the relation between the new Church and Judaism.

6. Name the main groups of scriptures in the New Testament, and explain the process by which the four Gospel accounts were written and compiled.

7. Explain the major doctrinal and organizational developments in Christianity from the time of Clement until the division between the Roman and Orthodox Churches. You should be able to discuss, in particular, the role of Greek philosophy in the formation of doctrine, the major heresies the Church addressed, the councils at Nicea and Chalcedon, and the significance of monasticism.

8. Give a description of the theology of Thomas Aquinas, examine the role reason plays in his thought, and detail at least one of his arguments for the existence of God.

9. Analyze the role and significance of the Reformation movement, describe the major distinctions between the three major streams of this movement and name the major points of contention between the Protestant reformers and the Roman Catholic Church.

10. Describe the development of Christianity from the time of the Reformation until the present day. You should be able to discuss and illustrate the nature of Christian missionary endeavors, the role of Christianity among American Blacks, and liberation theology.

11. Discuss and write about the Christian Worldview; in particular, the Christian view of The Absolute, the universe, the human role in the universe, the fundamental problem and resolution for human beings, community and ethics, rituals and symbols, life after death, and other religious traditions.

12. Cite and discuss at least three issues that confront and challenge contemporary Christianity.

13. Define the concept of resurrection of the dead, analyze how this concept was developed and expressed in Christian writings, and contrast this view of immortality with the view found in other religious traditions.

PART TWO   TERMS AND INDIVIDUALS

A) Terms and Concepts

Jerusalem temple
Son of David
the Christ
Church of Holy Sepulcher
Orthodox
Protestant
Kingdom of God
Pharisees
Messiah
Holy Communion
Golgotha
resurrection
Pentecost
apostles
Gentiles
agape
Council of Nicea
canon
heretics
allegorical method
homoousia
heresies
Monophysites
Trinity
economia
grace
Dominicans
deacon
bishop
excommunicate
Iconoclastic Controversy
icon
crusades
Ninety-Five Theses
Peace of Augsburg

rabbi
King of the Jews
Christianity
Son of God
Roman Catholic
miracles
Samaritan
Mosaic law
Palm Sunday
Zealots
Easter
Kingdom of God
Holy Spirit
kerygma
Judaizers
catechumen
New Testament
sacraments
Christian Platonists
Logos
ecumenical
Adoptionists
Council of Chalcedon
persona
filioque
stigmata
Coptic Christianity
presbyter
Bishop of Rome (Pope)
iconostasis
iconodule
Scholasticism
Protestant
indulgences
Council of Trent

sacraments
Eucharist
Marriage
Penance
Reform Movement
humanist
Presbyterian churches
Society of Jesus (Jesuit)
Congregationalism
Methodist churches
Mennonites
Deism
World Council of Churches
Second Vatican Council
liberals
the Incarnation
Atonement
theodicy
The Mass
Good Friday
Hell
anno Domini

Baptism
Confirmation
Holy Orders
Anointing of the Sick
Lutheranism
Church of England
Society of Friends (Quakers)
Nestorian Christianity
Baptist churches
Brethren
Great Awakening
Theism
First Vatican Council
liberation theology
fundamentalists
Resurrection of the Dead
mystery
tithing
Maundy Thursday
Christmas
Heaven

B) Individuals

Jesus of Nazareth
King Herod
Shammai
Mary
Elijah
Pilate
Joseph of Arimathea
Paul (Saul of Taurus)
Joseph Barnabas
Nero
Perpetua
Saturus
Revocatus
Origen
Bishop Methodius
Arius
St. Thomas Aquinas
St. John Chrysostom
St. Francis of Assisi
St. John of the Cross

John the Baptist
Hillel
Peter
Joseph
Judas
Barabbas
St. Augustine
Stephen
Peter
Constantine
Felicitas
Saturninus
Clement
Pantaenus
Ambrose
Athanasius
Tertullian
St. Benedict of Nursia
St. Dominic
St. Teresa of Avila

James
Patriarch Cerularius
Prince Vladimir of Kiev
St. Anselm
Michelangelo
Martin Luther
Pope Leo X
John Knox
George Fox
Francis Xavier
Matteo Ricci
Jonathan Edwards
Juan Luis Segundo
James H. Cone
Rosemary Radford Ruether
Karl Barth
Cotton Mather
John Woolman
Walter Rauschenbusch
Mother Teresa

Pope Leo IX
Pope Gregory the Great
Albert the Great
Pope Urban II
Pope Julius II
Tetzel
John Calvin
Henry VIII
St. Ignatius Loyola
Alessandro Valignano
George Whitefield
Pope John XXIII
Gustavo Gutierrez
J. Deotis Roberts
Albert Schweitzer
Emile Brunner
St. Irenaeus
Henry Ward Beecher
Martin Luther King

C) Texts

Acts of the Apostles
New Testament
Gospel of Mark
Gospel of Luke
Q (Quelle)
Thessalonians
Galatians
Philippians
Colossians
Timothy
Peter
John
Hebrews
apocalyptic literature
De Principiis
Summa Contra Gentiltes
Vulgate
Spiritual Exercises

canon
gospels
Gospel of Matthew
Gospel of John
epistles
Corinthians (I,II)
Romans
Philemon
Ephesians
Titus
James
Jude
Revelation of John
manuscripts of Nag Hammadi
The Confessions
Summa Theologica
Institutes of the Christian Rel
Constitutions

D) Individuals and Terms From Other Traditions

Judaism
Rabbi Hillel

Islam
Rabbi Shammai

Passover	Hellenism
Alexander the Great	Plato
Platonism	Philo
Plotinus	Aristotle
Toyotomi Hideyoshi	Oda Nobunaga
Mao Tse-tung	John Locke
René Descartes	Voltaire
Marxism	Manichaeanism
Nicholas Copernicus	Galileo Galilei
Sir Isaac Newton	Charles Darwin
Mohandas K. Gandhi	

PART THREE   GUIDED REVIEW

1. The Christian holiday of Easter is the day when Christians believe _____.

2. When Jesus met his cousin John the Baptist in the gospel accounts what happened was _____
_____.

3. Besides teaching his followers, Jesus also often _____
_____.

4. Jesus's attitude towards the Mosaic Law could be described as _____.

5. Many of Jesus's followers addressed him as _____, which meant _____.

6. When Jesus taught he often used a type of tale called _____.

7. The term "Messiah" means _____.

8. Many Christians believe that when Jesus and his followers ate their last supper together Jesus instituted _____
_____.

9. The New Testament contains accounts that after Jesus rose from the dead his followers saw _____.

10. Pentecost was the day that _____

_____ .

11. Although Paul became the greatest champion of the new Jesus movement, for a time he _____ .

12. A major controversy for the early Church was the questions of whether Gentiles had to _____

_____ .

13. Paul's attitude towards the body and sex was _____

_____ .

14. Roman Catholics believe that the first bishop of Rome was _____ .

15. _____ and _____ were the young mother and her slave who choose martyrdom over renouncing their faith.

16. The persecution of the Christians in the Roman Empire ended when _____ made Christianity a legal religion.

17. Scholars believe that the earliest of the four Gospel accounts to be written was _____ .

18. The Gospel accounts of Matthew and Luke, many scholars believe, were based in part on the writings _____ and _____ .

19. The Gospels were probably written sometime after _____ .

20. The oldest texts in the New Testament are those written by _____ , which are in the form of _____ .

21. A major influence upon early Christian thinkers such as Origen was _____ . The method that many of these thinkers used is termed the _____ method.

22. One teaching of Origen that was rejected later by the Church was his belief that _____ .

23. The council at Nicea rejected the position of the Arians who believed that _____.

24. The Greek term <u>homoousia</u> means _____ _____.

25. The Council of Chalcedon took the position that Jesus was _____.

26. The Roman Catholic and Orthodox traditions disagreed over the question of whether the Holy Spirit _____ _____.

27. Augustine and Pelagius disagreed over the question of _____.
Augustine's position was _____.

28. Three famous religious orders were those of the _____, the _____ and the _____.

29. One difference between the Roman Catholic and Orthodox traditions is their use of religious symbols; the Orthodox tradition makes great use of _____.

30. The approach that developed in the schools of France in the eleventh century and that applied logic to theological questions was called _____.

31. Thomas Aquinas believed that some truths concerning God could be accepted by using either _____ or _____.

32. Despite the fact that the Crusades were supposed to attack Muslims, in fact much violence was also committed against _____ and_____.

33. The three main divisions from Rome during the Reformation were those of _____, _____ and _____.

34. According to the Roman Catholic Church the sources of authority were _____ _____. Luther argued that the main source of authority was _____.

35. Henry VIII separated the Church of England from the Roman Catholic Church not over issues of _____, but rather over issues of _____.

36. The spiritual revival that occurred in the American Colonies around 1726-1740 was called _____.

37. Two of the reforms that came out of the Second Vatican Council were _____ and _____.

38. The recent Christian theology that stresses the importance of the Church preaching to and supporting the poor and oppressed is called _____.

39. Although Christians believe that God appears in three persons, they also believe there is _____ God. This is called the doctrine of the _____.

40. Many Christians emphasize that man and nature have been fundamentally flawed ever since _____.

41. A theodicy is any theory that _____
_____.

42. In general, one becomes a Christian through the ritual of
_____.

43. John Woolman, Henry Ward Beecher and Walter Rauschenbusch all were similar in that they _____.

44. Roman Catholic worship tends to emphasize the _____ _____ , while Protestant services are more likely to emphasize _____.

45. A sacrament could be defined as _____
_____.

46. Regarding the issue of life after death, Culmann draws a distinction between the Greek belief in _____, and the Christian belief in _____. The Christian belief is that _____
_____.

PART FOUR   ANALYZING TEXTS

Below are three texts that were not in the textbook.
The texts, however, do contain ideas and concepts with
which you should be familiar after reading the textbook.
Read each text carefully, and try to analyze each by
answering the following questions: What are the main
ideas in the text?   What viewpoint or viewpoints might
the author of the text represent? Is it possible to
identify the specific thinker, discipline, movement,
tradition or work from which the text derives? What
intellectual, literary, social, cultural or historical
influences are reflected in the text? For each of your
conclusions, try to point to specific evidence in the
text (e.g. terms, ideas, arguments, writing style, etc.)
which supports your conclusion. Be careful that your
conclusions do not exceed the evidence upon which they
rest.

TEXT ONE

Hence has originated that detestable tyranny of the
clergy over the laity, in which, trusting to the
corporal unction by which their hands are consecrated,
to their tonsure, and to their vestments, they not only
set themselves above the body of lay Christians, who
have been anointed with the Holy Spirit, but almost look
upon them as dogs, unworthy to be numbered in the Church
along with themselves. . .How if they were compelled to
admit that we all, so many as have been baptized, are
equally priests? We are so in fact, and it is only a
ministry which has been entrusted to them, and with our
consent. They would then know that they have no right
to exercise command over us, except so far as we
voluntarily allow it. [1]

TEXT TWO

Learn a lesson from the fig-tree. When its tender
shoots appear and are breaking into leaf, you know that
summer is near. In the same way, when you see all this
happening, you may know that the end is near, at the
very door. I tell you this: the present generation will

live to see it all. Heaven and earth will pass away; my words will never pass away. [2]

TEXT THREE

But now, quite independently of Law, God's justice has been brought to light. The Law and the Prophets both bear witness to it; it is God's way of righting wrong, effective through faith in Christ for all who have such faith - all without distinction. For all alike have sinned, and are deprived of the divine splendour, and all are justified by God's free grace alone, through his act of liberation in the person of Christ Jesus. For God designed him to be the means of expiating sin by his sacrificial death, effective through faith. [3]

PART FIVE   SELF-TEST

A) Definitions and Descriptions - Write your own definition or description of each of the following terms, individuals or texts. After completing the self-test, check your answer with the definition or description given in the textbook.

1. agape _____
_____
_____.

2. indulgences _____
_____
_____.

3. Great Awakening _____
_____
_____.

4. Judaizer _____
_____
_____.

5. resurrection _____
_____
_____.

6. liberation theology _____
_____
_____.

7. Logos _____
_____
_____.

8. icon _____
_____
_____.

9. catechumen _____
_____
_____.

10. allegorical method _____
_____
_____.

B) Multiple Choice

1. Which Roman Emperor made Christianity a legal religion?

   a. Nero
   b. Claudius
   c. Constantine
   d. Domitian

2. The final supper that Jesus had with his followers became
   the basis for what sacrament?

   a. Euchrist
   b. Confirmation
   c. Baptism
   d. Marriage.

3. Which of the following is not one of the canonical
   gospels?

   a. Luke
   b. John
   c. Mark
   d. Thomas

4. The Society of Friends was founded by

    a. William Penn
    b. Ignatius Loyola
    c. Francis Xavier
    d. George Fox

5. Which of the following would Luther recognize as a sacrament?

    a. Confirmation
    b. Holy Orders
    c. Baptism
    d. Marriage

6. The group that believed that Christ was the highest and best creature made by God was the

    a. Arians
    b. Adoptionists
    c. Monophysites
    d. Pelagians

7. The Christian Church is believed to have begun on the day called

    a. Christmas.
    b. Pentecost.
    c. Easter.
    d. Good Friday.

8. Which of the following is the traditional Christian position concerning life after death?

    a. Immortality of the soul
    b. Reincarnation
    c. Resurrection of the dead.
    d. Resurrection of the spirit only.

9. The founder of the Jesuit order was

    a. St. Francis.
    b. St. Benedict.
    c. St. Ignatius Loyola.
    d. St. Thomas Aquinas.

10. The type of story that Jesus often used in his teachings is

    a. Folk tales.
    b. Myths.
    c. Legends.
    d. Parables.

C) <u>True-False</u>

T   F   1. The followers of Jesus during his lifetime called Jesus by the title "rabbi."

T   F   2. St. Thomas Aquinas shifted Christian theology from Aristotelianism to Platonism.

T   F   3. The term "Messiah" means "the annointed of God."

T   F   4. Prior to the Second Vatican Council all Roman Catholic translations of the Bible were done from the Septuagint.

T   F   5. Many scholars believe that the Gospel to Matthew was written by reference to "Q".

T   F   6. Jesus of Nazareth rejected completely Mosaic Law.

T   F   7. The Christian term "Kerygma" refers to the healing power of Jesus.

T   F   8. The Council of Chalcedon sided with the Monophysites on the question concerning the nature of Jesus Christ.

T   F   9. John Calvin stressed that humans can not save themselves through doing good deeds.

T   F   10. The Gospel According to John is usually viewed as giving an account of the life of Jesus independent from the other gospels.

PART SIX   ESSAY AND DISCUSSION QUESTIONS

1. Compare Martin Luther's and John Calvin's view of the salvation process and the role of the Church to the Roman Catholic view.

2. Describe Paul's view of sex, love and women. What influence do you think Paul's position on these questions had on later Christian thought?

3. Compare and contrast the view of Mosaic Law in Rabbinic Judaism, in Jesus's teachings and in Paul's teachings (refer to Text Three above.) For each of them, how does Torah figure in God's plan for mankind? Is Paul's position the same as the position of Jesus?

4. Explain the process by which the gospels were formed. How might this process raise issues concerning the nature and authority of scripture?

5. Summarize Aquinas's attempt to prove the existence of God through an analysis of motion. Is Aquinas's argument a sound one? Why or why not? What does an argument of this type illustrate about how Aquinas believed man could approach God?

6. Explain the development of Christology (the study of who Jesus was) from the New Testament writings until the Council of Chalcedon.

PART SEVEN   CONFRONTING ISSUES AND ANSWERS

   The "Confronting Issues and Answers" section of the chapter on Hinduism asked how Hindus could adjust their views on the changing roles of women. This is a question that confronts all of the major world religions. A variety of factors, however, make this an especially contentious issue in Christianity. The multitude of different denominations and sects within Christianity means that there can be no unified response to this issue; different groups will address the issue in different ways. The greater overall status of women in Western culture leads many women with Christian beliefs to demand that they achieve complete equality with

men in the Church. In addition, according to the
interpretation of many Christians, there are passages in the
New Testament that appear to give women a different, and,
perhaps, lesser role than men. For example, Paul exhorted:
"Wives, be subject to your husbands; that is your Christian
duty. Husbands, love your wives and do not be harsh with
them"(Colossians III:18).

Think about the role of women in Christianity in reference
to two questions. First, what might be the sources of
authority that different Christians might use to resolve this
question? Which Christian branches might emphasize which
sources? Might there be problems in determining exactly what
the position of an authority might be on the role of women?
For example, if one held that the Bible is the ultimate
authority, what problems might there be in determining what
the Bible has to say on the role of women? Second, to what
degree can the role of women change as the social and
historical circumstances change? Could the proper Christian
role for women at the time of Jesus be different than the
proper Christian role at the beginning of the Twenty-First
century? Will ones answer to this question be dependent on
ones view of the source of authority?

PART EIGHT   AN ESSAY FOR DEEPER CONSIDERATION

Essay Question

Compare the Christian belief in resurrection of the dead
to Plato's belief in immortality of the soul, and the Hindu
belief in Atman and reincarnation. Where are these beliefs
similar and where are they different?

Tips for Answering

In a previous "Essay for Deeper Consideration" section you
were asked to write a comparison essay. A number of tips
were given on how you might structure a comparison essay. In
many cases, however, before you can present a comparison to
your readers, you may need to consider a number of related or
underlying issues. This essay question illustrates some of
these issues, and how you could address them in your essay.
You would not want to raise all these questions in any one
essay; you rather should consider how each relates to the

thesis around which you want to structure your writing.

You might decide to begin by defining and clarifying each of the three concepts of life after death. After all, before you can compare the three views you will need to explicate each view for your readers. Each of the three positions is a complex belief. The Hindu position on reincarnation, for example, can not be understood apart from the theory of the Atman. Within the course of explaining reincarnation you would need to define "Atman" and explain the role of Atman in Hindu belief. Similarly, in order to understand the concept of resurrection of the dead it is necessary to address the issue of what is resurrected. Theoretically, one could believe in the resurrection of different elements of the human being (e.g. body, mind, spirit, some combination of these). According to Christian understanding, what is the nature of the resurrected person? Furthermore, what does the answer to this question reveal about the Christian view of the nature of the human person? Obviously, in your essay you can not address fully every relevant topic. However, you will need to be aware of these issues, and will need to decide which of these questions need to be raised and answered in the course of explicating each positions.

You might also address the issue of how ideas from different cultures can be compared. The essay question might assume that a comparison between these three positions is unproblematic. Is this the case? These three views were adopted in three very different cultural milieus: the early Christian movement, Greece and India. Language, ideas, worldviews - all these are shaped by ones culture. In each case, how was the position on life after death reflective of and shaped by the culture? A further aspect of this question is the degree to which apparent differences in the three positions merely reflect different ways different cultures express the same idea. To what degree are the divergences between these three positions differences in the way in which the beliefs are expressed, and to what degree are they differences in what the beliefs express? Finally, you might raise the more fundamental issue of the validity of such a comparison. Can each position only be understood and analyzed in terms of its own worldview and culture? This is a fairly radical position, but you might believe that the issue needs to be examined prior to a comparison of the views.

PART NINE   PROJECTS FOR DEVELOPING RELIGIOUS EMPATHY

1. Many Christians find in "The Sermon on the Mount" one of
   the most beautiful and clearest descriptions of the
   Christian life. In this passage Jesus gives his closest
   disciples both general values and principles to live by,
   and specific injunctions and prohibitions. Many scholars
   believe that the author of The Gospel According to Matthew
   gathered together talks given by Jesus at different times,
   and combined them in this one passage. Scholars have also
   commented on the manner in which this gospel distinguishes
   between teachings for the public, and teachings for the
   disciples. The Sermon would seem to belong to the latter
   category. Finally, the fact that the author chooses to
   portray Jesus as giving this speech on a hill could be an
   attempt to draw a connection between Moses, Mount Sinai
   and the Law, on the one hand, and Jesus, the hill and a
   new view of Law. All these factors suggest that for the
   author of this gospel, and for Christians since, Jesus's
   talk should be a guide for Christians on how to live.

   Read the Sermon on the Mount in a modern translation of
   The Gospel According to Matthew (Matthew V-VII). (You
   might also want to compare this version of the Sermon with
   the version found in The Gospel According to Luke
   beginning at VI:17.) What do you think Jesus is asking of
   his followers? Imagine that you were trying to live
   according to what Jesus says in this passage, how would
   you have to live your life? What changes, if any, would
   you have to make in your life? Are there things that you
   do or believe in with which Jesus would disagree? Try to
   imagine one day lived in accord with this sermon.
   Specifically, what would such a day be like?

2. A religion expresses itself in its houses of worship, both
   inside and outside. Church buildings are, in part, the
   attempt to express in architecture some of the beliefs of
   Christianity. Close observation and analysis of different
   church buildings can tell you a lot about Christian
   beliefs. It can also serve as an indication of how
   different denominations and groups see the Christian
   message.

Together with a fellow student or a friend, compile a list
of different churches in your town or city. Include on
your list any famous churches, and any church buildings
that you know to be architecturally important. If your
city has a Roman Catholic or Episcopal Cathedral (the
principal church of the bishop's see) include it on your
list. Try to put on your list churches that reflect a
wide variety of Christian denominations (a meeting house
of the Society of Friends, a Unitarian church, a Baptist
church, a Black Pentecostal storefront church, etc.) Your
selection will be influenced by the diversity of religious
groups in your town, and the physical proximity of the
different buildings.

After you have compiled your list, take a walking tour
with your companion. When you get to each building notice
the particulars of the architecture: What is the physical
location of the building? What is the relation between
the physical location of the building, and the size and
scope of the building? How would you describe the
building's shape? Are there any ornaments on the outside
of the building, and if so, what are they? Would you
describe the building as simple, or ornate? Out of which
materials is the building made, and how does this
influence the aesthetic of the building? After you have
noted these features, consider how they might reflect the
Christian message as this church interprets it: What
values might a simple building or an ornate building
express? What message might be given by putting a church
on top of a hill? Would this differ from building a
church in amongst homes and businesses? How could you
express architecturally the concept of being open to all
people? How could you express the concept of the
importance of God?

3. For Christians a church is more than a building. A church
    is also the community of believers in Christ. You might
    want to visit, with a friend, a number of different
    Christian congregations and observe their worship and
    fellowship. If you feel you would like to do this, try to
    visit at least two congregations from different parts of
    the Christian spectrum. If you are going to visit a large
    urban church, you will probably not have to talk to the
    minister or priest beforehand. However, if you plan to
    visit a small congregation, it would be best to contact

the minister prior to your actual visit. Explain that you
are taking a course in World Religions, and as part of a
class project you would like to observe a variety of
Christian denominations. You should also communicate
that, while you are a student of religion, you are not
seeking to join any particular group. If the minister
does not feel comfortable with your visit, you should not
visit that particular group.

When you visit each service, observe how each group
expresses its religious beliefs in worship. What are the
practices of each group? What is the relation (both
physically and organizationally) of the clergy or leader
to the group as a whole? What appear to be the most
important portions of the service? If you were
summarizing the service like a drama, when does the climax
occur? What is the emotional feeling during the service:
excited, calm, reflective, anxious? What conclusions can
you draw concerning each group based on your observation
of their religious rituals?

ANSWER KEY TO SELF-TEST

B) Multiple Choice

1. c   6. a
2. a   7. b
3. d   8. c
4. d   9. c
5. c   10. d

C) True-False

1. T   6. F
2. F   7. F
3. T   8. F
4. F   9. T
5. T   10. T

Notes

[1]Martin Luther, "On the Babylonish Captivity of the Church," First Principles of the Reformation, trans. H. Wace and C. A. Buchheim (Philadelphia: Lutheran Publication Society; 1885) 232.

[2]The Gospel According to Mark, XIII:28-31, The New English Bible (Oxford: Oxford University Press, 1970)

[3]St. Paul, The Letter of Paul to the Romans, III: 21-25, The New English Bible (Oxford: Oxford University Press, 1970).

Chapter 9

Text. Chap 10 376

ISLAM

PART ONE   LEARNING OBJECTIVES

Doing these exercises, in conjunction with reading the
textbook, should help you to achieve the following
objectives. Read them and see how many you already have
mastered; then study the following terms and concepts, and
work through the exercises. After you have completed all the
exercises, return to this section and review the objectives
again.

You should be able to:

1. Describe the Muslim <u>hajj</u>, and indicate its significance
   for Islam.

2. Relate the life of Muhammad, explain his role as prophet
   and messenger in Islam, and illustrate the importance of
   Muhammad as a role-model for Muslims.

3. Explain and analyze the role of the Quran for Islam, and compare and contrast Islam's view of the Quran to the view of scripture in other religious traditions.

4. Analyze the organizational development of Islam during the time of the first four caliphs, and indicate how events during this period influenced Islam at a later date

5. Describe and analyze the differences between the Shia and the Sunni branches of Islam, and indicate the effect this split has on the Islamic world today.

6. Discuss the notion of the Sharia, name and explain at least four standards that can be used to interpret law, and name and describe the four different schools of Islamic legal interpretation.

7. Cite some of the Greek influences on Islam, and illustrate how some of these influences were reflected in Islamic philosophy.

8. Examine the role of mysticism in Islam, in particular, discussing the Sufi movement, and orthodox Islam's reaction to this movement.

9. Summarize the position of al-Ghazali, and indicate his influence upon subsequent Islamic thought and practice.

10. Discuss the history of Islam's relation to other religions, including the relation between Muhammad and the Jewish population in Medina, the Crusades, Islam's influence on Medieval Christian theologians, and contemporary relations between Islam and other religions.

11. Examine and write about the problem of Islam and Modernism, citing some examples of different Islamic responses to this problem.

12. Discuss and write about the Islamic Worldview; in particular, the Islamic view of the Absolute, the universe, the human role in the universe, the fundamental problem and resolution for human beings, community and ethics, rituals and symbols, life after death, and other religions.

13. Analyze and synthesize various views on revelation in
    Islam and other religions, and formulate in writing a
    comprehensive understanding of revelation.

PART TWO   TERMS AND INDIVIDUALS

A) Terms and Concepts

Islam	Mecca (Makkah)
Allah	Haram Mosque
Ka'bah	kiswah
angel Gabriel	ihram
Medina (Yathrib)	hajj
hajji	hajjiyah
Quraysh tribe	hanif
jinn	Ummayads
house of Hashim	Hijrah
sheik	ansar
muhajirun	Khazraj
Aws	Hawazin
Thaquf	monotheism
Shahada	zagat
Ramadan	Tawhid
salat	mosque
rakas	muezzin
Shaitan	jizyah
surah	hadith
caliph	Shia
Sunni	Kharijites
imam	Twelvers
Zaydites	Ismailis
Mogul Empire	dhimmi
Sharia	ijma
ulama	giyas
Hanifite school	ray
Malikite school	Shafiite school
Hanbalite	Murjites
Mutazilites	Sufis
peoples of the Book	Crusades
Saladin	Taj Mahal
madrasas	Wahhabi
Salifiya	pan-Islam
al-Azhar	ummah
Muslim Brotherhood	Iblis

Adam
Satan
Id al-Fitr
Black Muslim
prophet

Eve
mihrab
purdah
revelation (<u>wahy</u>)
messenger

B) <u>Individuals</u>

Muhammad
Hagar
Sarah
Abdullah
Halimah
Khadijah
Ruqayyah
Katima
Zayd Ibn Harithah
Abu Bakr
Uthman Ibn Affan
Abu Sufyan
Zaynab Bint al-Harith
Abu Bakr
Umar
Muawiyah
Husayn
Zayd
Musa al-Kazim
Akbar
Hanbal
al-Ashari
Ibn Arabi
al-Din Rumi
al-Farabi
Ibn Arabi
Ibn Rushd (Averroës)
Muhammad Ibn Abd al-Wahhab
Jamil-al-Din al-Afghani
Muhammad Abduh
Amir Ali
Abul Ala Mawdudi
Benazir Bhutto
Sayyid Qutb
Hasni Mubarak
Yasir Arafat
Malcolm X

Abraham
Ishmael
Isaac
Aminah
Abu Talib
Zaynab
Umm-Khulthum
Waraqa Ibn-Nawfal
Ali
Khalid Ibn Said
Aishah
Khalid Ibn al-Walid
Zayd Ibn Thabit
Aishah
Uthman
Hasan
Muhammad al-Mahdi
Ismail
Usamah
Babur
al-Shafi
al-Ghazali
Rabia
al-Hallaj
Ibn Sina
Beha-ed-Din
Shah Jahan
Rashid Rida
Abd al-Hamid II
Sayyid Ahmad Khan
Sir Muhammad Iqbal
Zia ul-Haq
Gammel Abdel Nasser
Anwar Sadat
Muammar al-Qaddafi
Elijah Muhammad

C) <u>Texts</u>

Quran   Sunnah
<u>The Spirit of Islam</u>   <u>Green Book</u>
hadiths

D) <u>Individuals and Terms from Other Traditions</u>

Judaism   Christianity
Byzantine   Charles Martel
Buddhism   Neoplatonism
Gnosticism   materialists
naturalists   theists
Plato   Aristotle
New Testament   Son of God
Trinity   patriarch of Constantinople
Pope Urban II   Alexius I
Frederick II   Holy Roman Empire
Richard I   Maimonides
St. Thomas Aquinas   Albertus Magnus
Sikhism   Nicolaus Copernicus
Charles Darwin   Henri Bergson
Fredrich Nietzsche   Alfred North Whitehead
Greek Orthodox Christianity   Israel

PART THREE   GUIDED REVIEW

1. The holy city that all Muslims face in prayer _____
times a day is _____.

2. According to Islam the final prophet of God is _____
_____.

3. The Ka'bah is a _____.
It is usually covered with a _____.

4. Inside the Ka'bah is a _____. Muslims
believe that this was given by _____ to _____
_____.

5. During the time one participates in the <u>hajj</u> one is in a
state of _____. A male who completes the <u>hajj</u> is
called a _____, a female a _____.

6. At the time Muhammad was born, inside the Ka'bah there were _____.

7. _____ was the wife of Muhammad, and his counselor.

8. While meditating in a cave, Muhammad was given a message from _____, delivered by _____. At first Muhammad was afraid that he was _____ _____.

9. The <u>Hijrah</u> was _____.

10. The city to which Muhammad moved, Yathrib, is today called _____. It was while he was here that friction began to develop between Muhammad and his followers, and _____.

11. The five requirements that are made of every Muslim are:
a) _____, b) _____
_____, c) _____
_____, d) _____
and e) _____.

12. <u>Tawhid</u> is _____.

13. Islam rejects the Christian beliefs that _____
_____.

14. The two chief sources of authority in Islam are, first, the Quran, and after this, _____.

15. One difference between the <u>Shia</u> and the <u>Sunni</u> is over their understanding of _____. According to the Shia, Ali was the first _____.

16. The group known as the Twelvers believe that _____
_____. They believe that the <u>Mahdi</u> will _____.

17. The Muslim expansion into Europe was finally turned back by _____.

18. The term <u>Sharia</u> means _____.
According to different schools, this might involve
_____, _____, _____,
and even _____.

19. The legal school known as the Hanbalite School could be
described as _____. It is prevalent
in the country of _____.

20. The position of the Mutazilites was _____
_____.

21. The name "Sufi" is taken from _____.

22. The Persian Sufi al-Hallaj was _____
_____.

23. al-Ghazali thought that Aristotle and Plato _____
_____.

24. According to Ibn Arabi, everything that we experience is
_____.

25. While Jews and Christians were not forced to convert to
Islam, they were made to _____.

26. The Crusades were undertaken with the goal of _____
_____.

27. Ibn Rushd is better known in the West as _____.
He was famous for his commentaries on the works of _____
_____, which were studied by _____.

28. The Taj Mahal was built as a _____.

29. The movement known as Wahhabi stresses _____
_____.

30. Amir Ali argued that Muhammad was _____
_____.

31. Sir Muhammad Iqbal is noteworthy for both _____
_____ and for _____
_____.

32. The views of _____ on the Islamic State were expressed in <u>The Green Book</u>.

33. One of the most important recent events in the Islamic world was the return of _____ to Iran in 1979.

34. Islam's views on the issue of The Absolute can be described as a position of _____. For Islam the only God is _____.

35. Islam interprets the story of Adam and Eve to mean _____
_____.

36. The term for a Muslim community is _____.

37. Islam's view on divorce is _____.

38. Mosques have a <u>mihrab</u> so that _____.

39. Islam's view on life after death is _____
_____.

40. A. J. Arberry cites two types of revelation in the Quran, one is _____, and the other is
_____.

PART FOUR   ANALYZING TEXTS

Below are three texts that were not in the textbook. The texts, however, do contain ideas and concepts with which you should be familiar after reading the textbook. Read each text carefully, and try to analyze each by answering the following questions: What are the main ideas in the text?   What viewpoint or viewpoints might the author of the text represent? Is it possible to identify the specific thinker, discipline, movement, tradition or work from which the text derives? What intellectual, literary, social, cultural or historical influences are reflected in the text? For each of your conclusions, try to point to specific evidence in the text (e.g. terms, ideas, arguments, writing style, etc.) which supports your conclusion. Be careful that your conclusions do not exceed the evidence upon which they rest.

TEXT ONE

Know that the key of happiness is following the <u>Sunna</u> and imitating God's Apostle in all his goings out and comings in, in his movements and times of quiescence, even in the manner of his eating, his deportment, his sleep and his speech. I do not say that concerning his manners in matters of religious observances alone, because there is no reason to neglect the traditions which have come down concerning them: nay, that has to do with all matters of use and wont, for in that way unrestricted following arises. . . Muhammad b. Aslam used not to eat a melon because the manner in which God's Apostle ate it had not been transmitted to him.[1]

TEXT TWO

Say: "O mankind, I am Allah's messenger to you all,
Of Him to whom belongeth the kingdom of the heavens
    and of the earth.

There is no god but He.
He giveth life and he causeth to die.
Believe then in Allah, and in His messenger,
The <u>ummi</u> prophet, who himself believeth in Allah
    and His words, and follow him;
Haply so ye will be guided. [2]

TEXT THREE

I died as a mineral and became a plant,
I died as a plant and rose to animal,
I died as animal and I was man.
Why should I fear? When was I less by dying?
Yet once more I shall die as man, to soar
With angels blest; but even from angelhood
I must pass on: all except God doth perish.
When I have sacrificed my angel soul,
I shall become what no mind e'er conceived.
Oh, let me not exist! for Non-existence
Proclaims in organ tones, "To Him we shall return." [3]

PART FIVE   SELF-TEST

A) <u>Definitions and Descriptions</u> - Write your own definition or description of each of the following terms, individuals or texts. After completing the self-test, check your answer with the definition or description given in the textbook.

1. Tawhid _____
_____
_____.

2. Ramadan _____
_____
_____.

3. Wahhabi _____
_____
_____.

4. jinn _____
_____
_____.

5. hajj _____
_____
_____.

6. surah _____
_____
_____.

7. imam _____
_____
_____.

8. Shia _____
_____
_____.

9. zagat _____
_____
_____.

10. Islam _____

_____

_____.

B) Multiple Choice

1. Which of the following is <u>not</u> mentioned as one of the
   considerations in determining <u>Sharia</u>?

   a. Quran
   b. giyas
   c. ijma
   d. salat

2. According to <u>Shia</u> the first imam was

   a. Ali
   b. Abu Bakr
   c. Muawiyah
   d. Muhammad al-Mahdi al-Hujja

3. A male who has completed the pilgrimage to Mecca is called
   a

   a. hajj
   b. hajjiyah
   c. hajji
   d. ihram

4. A tradition of the prophet is called

   a. ijma.
   b. ulama.
   c. hadith.
   d. giya.

5. The tomb of Muhammad is located in

   a. Mecca.
   b. Medina.
   c. Baghdad.
   d. Jerusalem.

6. Muhammad was from the house of

   a. Ummayad.
   b. Quraysh.
   c. Hashim.
   d. Aws.

7. Which of these is not one of the Five Pillars of Islam?

   a. Pay a tax to the needy.
   b. Fast during Ramadan.
   c. Declare the Shahada.
   d. Read the Hadiths.

8. Which of the following is not mentioned as a difference between the Shiites and the Sunnis?

   a. The need for a pilgrimage to Mecca.
   b. The role of family relationships in choosing the successors to Muhammad.
   c. The role of the imam.
   d. The role of Ali.

9. The sacred building pilgrims walk around in Mecca is called

   a. Kiswah.
   b. Ka'bah.
   c. The Dome of the Rock.
   d. The Tomb of the Prophet.

10. The main Shia group is called

   a. Zaydites.
   b. Twelvers.
   c. Ismailis.
   d. Kharijites.

C) True-False

T F   1. The Hanbalite school is the most conservative of the legal schools.

T F   2. Friction between Muslims and Jews developed soon after Muhammad moved to Medina.

T F   3. The Zaidites believe that Husayn was the
                 proper fourth imam.

T F   4. Ibn Arabi conceived of God as the only
                 reality in the universe.

T F   5. The concept of Tawhid means that there are
                 gods who were created by Allah before he
                 created the earth.

T F   6. Muslims are required to pray in a group of
                 at least six people.

T F   7. The state of purity a Muslim must maintain
                 during the hajj is called ihram.

T F   8. Rabia was a famous Sufi mystic.

T F   9. The angel who delivered a message from God
                 Muhammad was the angel Moroni.

T F   10. Every Christian who lived in an area
                  conquered by Islam had to convert to Islam.

PART SIX   ESSAY AND DISCUSSION QUESTIONS

1. How would you describe Muhammad as a person? How would
   you contrast the type of person he was to the other major
   religious figures you have studied?

2. Address the issue of how Islam has viewed the relation
   between state and religion? What have been some of the
   attempts to realize an Islamic state, and how have these
   attempts differed?

3. Explain the differences between the Sunni and the Shia
   branches of Islam.

4. Describe the Sufi movement, and examine how it both
   differs from and resembles non-mystical forms of Islam.

5. What role has Greek philosophy played in Islamic thought?
   What aspects of Islamic thought might differ from the way

Greek thinkers like Aristotle and Plato looked at the world?

6. Examine the role that Islam has played in the Middle East since the 1967 Arab-Israeli War. What might be its future role in the region?

PART SEVEN   CONFRONTING ISSUES AND ANSWERS

All the major world religions are facing the challenge of adapting to the modern world. Scientific advances, demands on the part of women for greater equality, economic changes that are influencing the family and the individual - all these are factors each religion must address. In this regard, Islam is no different than most of the world's religions. Certain Islamic countries have strove to maintain or restore traditional Islamic values and practices; Saudi Arabia and Iran would be two such countries. The result has been a greater sense of frustration on the part of Muslims in those countries that want modernization, and a greater sense of determination on behalf of those who mean to resist it.

The question of modernization in Islam, however, is not a simple issue. Modernization in certain areas is seen as relatively unproblematic; modernization in other areas is strictly forbidden. As with many other religious traditions, moreover, the prohibitions in some areas are not rooted in scripture itself, but rather in tradition and interpretation. A recent example of this occurred in Saudi Arabia during the Fall of 1990 as this book was being written. Women are strictly forbidden to drive in Saudi Arabia. Influenced, perhaps, by the presence of American servicewomen driving in their country, a group of Saudi Arabian women got behind the wheels of their cars and drove through the streets of Riyadh. The women were stopped and taken into custody. They were later suspended from their teaching positions. Much of public opinion in the country condemned the women's actions. The fascinating aspect of this case, however, is the following. At the time of this incident it was not strictly illegal for the women to drive. Moreover, the Islamic scholars were in agreement that the Quran did not prohibit women from driving. Rather, the argument against women driving was based on tradition and a general belief in the proper role for women in an Islamic society. The factors

that the author of the textbook mentions in the section on
Sharia were coming into play.

Consider this incident from the standpoint of an Islamic
legal scholar. To what sources of authority might each side
of this issue appeal? Which sources would most likely be
given greater weight, and which might be give lesser or no
weight? How would the various schools of interpretation
differ in which sources they used? Would this specific
incident raise any special problems for reaching a decision
(eg. would it matter if it had occurred during a war?) Which
school of interpretation would best be able to make
adjustments to modernization?

PART EIGHT   AN ESSAY FOR DEEPER CONSIDERATION

Essay Question

Judaism, Christianity and Islam have each been called
"revealed-historical religions." Examine examples of "divine
revelation" in the Jewish, Christian and Islamic traditions.
Is it possible to synthesize the different examples of
revelation into a general Judeo-Christian-Islamic
understanding of revelation? What would such an
understanding look like?

Tips for Answering

This essay question assumes that you have already read the
chapters on Judaism and Christianity, and have discussed
those chapters in class. If this is not the case, you may
need to postpone working on this essay until you have studied
those traditions.

When you "analyze" something you break it down into its
component parts; when you "synthesize" something you draw
together parts in order to construct a new whole. The task
of "synthesis" is being defined in this essay assignment,
however, in a way that may differ from how it is defined in
some English classes. For example, a recent composition
textbook defines "synthesis" as when ". . . you take several
separate sources of information - a group of statements, a
collection of essays - and you analyze each individual point

of view and each way of looking at the topic. . . [you] incorporate them all in a new essay designed to represent a variety of opinion as well as your own point of view." [4] In one sense, of course, you are being asked to do some of this in this essay. You will need to select examples of God's revelation from each of the three traditions. You will also want to analyze each individual example in order to illuminate how each tradition understands the phenomenon of revelatory experiences. But you are also being asked to do something different than the type of synthesis mentioned in the quotation. You are not merely being asked to incorporate them into a new essay. You are being challenged to uncover common structures or elements in all three that would allow you to draw together a new understanding of revelation for all three traditions. Do the three traditions share a common view of revelation, and if so, what is that view? Answering this question should be your overall goal in writing the essay.

     Here are a few more suggestions to take into consideration. The textbook discusses the views of two scholars on revelation. You should not merely repeat either of these views in your essay, but they might provide you with models for a general theory of revelation. Also, when you choose your examples from each tradition, make sure you are choosing a "paradigm case". That is to say, each tradition contains unusual or controversial cases of revelatory experiences. An example in Islam might be the revelation to al-Hallaj. Such borderline cases have limited usefulness in deriving a general understanding of the concept. A widely accepted example, such as the revelation of the Quran to Muhammad, would be more useful. Finally, notice that the question leaves open the possibility that you will conclude that such a general understanding does not exists. If your analysis shows this, do not be afraid to argue that position.

PART NINE   PROJECTS FOR DEVELOPING RELIGIOUS EMPATHY

1. The projects suggested in this section of each chapter are not designed to convert you to any particular religion, or to encourage you to practice any religion. That is a matter for each individual to decide apart from a college course on religious studies. These projects, however, are formulated to get you to understand and empathize with

each of the religious traditions. One aspect of Islam
that many scholars have commented on is how rituals
structure time for a Muslim. Consider a few of the Five
Pillars, the obligations on all believers. The obligation
to witness is constant. Prayer structures each day into
five periods. The year revolves around Ramadan, and in a
sense, the lifetime revolves around the pilgrimage. Thus,
practice or action helps to define time as God's time.

To get a sense of how time can be structured, and how this
might change the way in which we see the world, try the
following. Choose five convenient times that are equally
distributed throughout the day and evening. For at least
three or four days try to stop whatever you are doing
during these times and spend five minutes on some quiet
reflection. If you normally pray in some way, you might
want to pray during these times. But if you do not pray,
then use them to examine a thought or to quietly think.
(Realize, of course, that for Islam, the crucial aspect of
these times is to witness to God. Any other use of the
times is significantly different.) Make them in some way
special times. When you have done this for a few days,
consider: How does doing this change the way in which you
go through your day? Is it a bother, one that takes time
away from your studies or partying? Or do you look
forward to it, as a break or a refreshing moment? Given
our society, are such breaks practical? Are they valuable
because they are not practical? What has this shown you
about Islamic practice?

2. The Middle East and Iran, and with it Islam, have been in
   the news constantly over the past ten years. Given the
   geo-political realities of the region, it would appear to
   be a safe prediction that Islam will continue to be a
   focus of attention for years to come. While many of the
   reasons for this attention are unfortunate ones, and may
   have little to do with the beliefs and practices of Islam
   itself, it does give you an opportunity to learn about the
   religion and the attitude of Americans towards it.

   Begin to keep a scrapbook of newspaper clippings dealing
   with Islam and countries that are predominantly Islamic.
   Cut out the relevant ones, and paste them in the book.
   Write a short reflection on each clipping. Try to focus
   on two issues. First, what do the accounts show you about

how Muslims view and try to achieve an Islamic state?
Which countries are mentioned as "Islamic" countries?
What do you think that means? What form of government do
these countries have (monarchy, democracy, oligarchy,
theocracy, etc.)? What view of an Islamic state do other
groups in the Middle East have? Second, what do these
articles show you about Americans' knowledge of and
opinion of Islam? Does it seem well-informed, unbiased?
Or does it seem ignorant and prejudiced? If you find
prejudice in some accounts, how is this manifested?
Should Americans try to learn more about Islam?

ANSWER KEY TO SELF-TEST

B) Multiple Choice

1. d   6. c
2. a   7. d
3. c   8. a
4. c   9. b
5. b   10. b

C) True-False

1. T   6. F
2. T   7. T
3. F   8. T
4. T   9. F
5. F   10. F

Notes

[1]Al-Ghazali, in James Robson, "Al-Ghazali and the Sunna", <u>The Muslim World</u>, Oct. 1955, Vol. 45, No. 4: 324-333.

[2]<u>Quran</u>, 7:157-8, quoted in Philip K. Hitti, <u>Islam: A Way of Life</u> (Chicago: Henery Regnery Company, 1970) 10.

[3]Al-Rumi, <u>Islam: A Way of Life</u>, Philip Hitti (Chicago: Henry Reqnery Company, 1970) 62-63.

[4]Brenda Spatt, <u>Writing from Sources</u>, 3rd Ed. (New York: St. Martin's Press, 1991) 223.

Chapter 10

MORE RECENT WORLD RELIGIONS

PART ONE - LEARNING OBJECTIVES

Doing these exercises, in conjunction with reading the textbook, should help you to achieve the following objectives. Read them and see how many you already have mastered; then study the following terms and concepts, and work through the exercises. After you have completed all the exercises, return to this section and review the objectives again.

You should be able to:

1. Compare the more recent world religions discussed in this chapter and illustrate what characteristics they have in common, and in what ways they are distinctive.

2. Name the major religious figures of the Baha'i movement, and recount their life stories and role in the development of the movement.

3. Discuss and write about the Baha'i Worldview, in particular, the Baha'i view of the Absolute, the universe, the human role in the universe, the fundamental problem and resolution for human beings, community and ethics, rituals and symbols, and the life after death.

4. Analyze the development of The Church of Latter-day Saints from the time of Joseph Smith up to today, including a discussion of The Book of Mormon, the organizational growth of the church, and Mormon political activity.

5. Discuss and write about the Mormon Worldview, in particular, the Mormon view of the Absolute, the universe and the human role in it, the fundamental problem and resolution for human beings, rituals and symbols, and life after death.

6. Relate the life story of Sun Myung Moon, and examine his role in the founding and development of the Unification Church.

7. Give a brief summary of the teachings of Sun Myung Moon as they are contained in the Divine Principle.

8. Discuss and write about the Worldview of Sun Myung Moon, including his view of the Absolute, the universe and the human role in it, the fundamental problem and resolution for human beings, rituals and symbols, community and ethics and life after death.

9. Discuss and illustrate the history of the movement known as Theosophy, including a discussion of the roles of H.P.Blavatsky, Colonel Olcott, Annie Besant, Krishnamurti and W. Q. Judge.

10. Explicate some of the theories and ideas of H.P.Blavatsky and Theosophy, including their view of The Absolute, the universe and the human role within it, the fundamental problem and resolution for human beings, life after death, and other religions.

11. Define "esoteric" and "exoteric", and discuss and evaluate Huston Smith's theory on the relation between these two aspects of religion.

12. Outline the history of the International Society for Krishna Consciousness, and show the role that Abhay Charan De played in the founding and development of this movement. You should also be able to relate a number of the beliefs of this movement.

13. Analyze how the religious movements discussed in this chapter grow out of or appropriated elements from previously existing movements, and how they added distinctive elements to their borrowed ideas and practices.

14. Give examples of practices within each of these movements that placed this movement outside the mainstream of religion in this country, and examine how each movement addressed these practices as it developed and matured.

15. Examine the issue of whether the term "religious cult" is a useful term in Religious Studies, and how this term might be applied to the movements discussed in this chapter.

PART TWO - TERMS AND INDIVIDUALS

A) Terms and Concepts

Baha'i
Unification Church
Hare Krishna movement
Twelvers
Universal House of Justice
Mormons
Cumorah
Thummim
Ether
polygamy
marriage
order of Aaron
First Presidency
Council of Seventy
baptism by proxy
reincarnation
Adepts
Point Loma

Church of Latter-day Saints
Theosophy
imam
Hands of the Cause
Mormon Tabernacle and Temple
Moroni
Urim
Babylonian captivity
gentiles
baptism
Lord's Supper
order of Melchizedek
Council of Twelve Apostles
genealogy
karma
spiritualism
Coulomb affair
Order of the Star of the East

raja yoga   Arcane School
Theosophical Society Inter.   United Lodge of Theosophists
Theosophical Society   Solar Deity
planetary spirits   esoteric
exoteric   ISKCON
Krishna   Gaudiya Vaisnava Maths
Vaisnavism   Krishna bhakti
kirtana   Vrndavana
New Vrindavan   mantra

B) Individuals

'Ali Muhammad (the Bab)   Baha'u'llah (Iman Mahdi)
Abdul-Baha   Shoghi Effendi Rabbani
Joseph Smith   Emma Smith
Brigham Young   Reverend Sun Myung Moon
Jesus Christ   John the Baptist
Elijah   Paul
H. P. Blavatsky   Colonel Henry Stell Olcott
Annie Besant   Eddy brothers
William Quan Judge   A. P. Sinnett
A. O. Hume   Charles Ledbetter
Krishnamurti   Katherine Tingley
Alice Bailey   Abhay Charan De (Bhaktivedanta)
Saraswati   Sri Caitanya

C) Texts

Bayan   Kitab-i-Aqdas
Kitab-i-Igan   The Book of Mormon
Divine Principle   The Temple Letters
Isis Unveiled   The Secret Doctrine
Stanzas of Dzyan   The Voice of Silence
Book of the Golden Precepts   The Theosophist
Back to the Godhead   Bhagavad Gita as It Is
Bhagavata Purana

D) Individual and Terms from Other Traditions

Buddhism   Hinduism
Islam   Christianity
Judaism   Queen Victoria
Ayatollah Khomeini   Methodist
Confucianism   Swami Dayanand Sarasvati
Arya Samaj   Neoplatonism

PART THREE   GUIDED REVIEW

1. The five religions examined in this chapter are _____
_____, _____,
_____, _____,
and _____.

2. Among the similarities among these five traditions is that
each _____ and each
_____.

3. The recent religion that seems the most influenced by
Islam is _____. The religions that
seem the most influenced by Indian religions are _____
_____ and _____. The
religions that seem the most influenced by Christianity are
_____ and _____.

4. The religious leader known as the Bab was _____
_____. The title "Bab" means _____.

5. The Twelvers were _____.

6. Baha'u'llah declared himself to be _____.

7. The Baha'i view of life after death is that _____
_____.

8. It was _____ who led Joseph Smith to a hill
where he found _____. This
was to be translated as _____.

9. According to Mormon belief the Native Americans (Indians)
are descended from _____.

10. Joseph Smith died when _____
_____.

11. Following the death of Joseph Smith, the leadership of
the movement was taken on by _____.

12. One Mormon practice that many Americans found
objectionable and that the church eventually renounced was
_____.

13. Baptism on behalf of the dead and marriage is possible only in _____, and is open only to _____.

14. Most Mormon males undertake _____ and become members of _____.

15. Because Mormons believe ones ancestors can be baptized, the study of _____ is very important in this religion.

16. The Unification Church was founded by _____.

17. Among the things for which the founder of the Unification Church is well-known are _____ and _____.

18. Moon believed that a new Messiah was necessary because of a failure on the part of _____. Because of this failure, _____ did not carry out God's plan and produce an ideal family.

19. The four-position foundation of which Moon writes consists of _____, _____, _____ and _____.

20. In its emphasis on the family, one can see the influence of _____ in Moon's thought.

21. Moon believes that the new Messiah will appear before the year _____.

22. The two people who were responsible for the founding of Theosophy were _____ and _____.

23. An early influence on the founders of Theosophy was the movement known as _____.

24. H. P. Blavatsky helped the Buddhists of Sri Lanka by _____.

25. The woman who was the leader of the Theosophy movement after Blavatsky was _____.

26. An important spiritual teacher who began within Theosophy, but eventually left the movement was _____.

27. The Absolute in Theosophy is seen as _____ _____.

28. Theosophy believes that each universe is an expression of _____.

29. The first stage after death, according to Theosophy, is _____.

30. Two changes that the author of the textbook mentions as possible reasons for the decline of interest in Theosophy are _____ and _____.

31. Schuon makes a distinction between _____ and _____.

32. The founder of ISKCON was _____.

33. The tradition out of which ISKCON grew was that of _____ as exemplified in _____.

34. One controversial practice of ISKCON was that of having its members _____.

35. Some members of ISKCON believe that they can belong to the movement and still _____.

PART FOUR   ANALYZING TEXTS

Below are two texts that were not in the textbook. The texts, however, do contain ideas and concepts with which you should be familiar after reading the textbook. Read each text carefully, and try to analyze each by answering the following questions: What are the main ideas in the text?   What viewpoint or viewpoints might the author of the text represent? Is it possible to identify the specific thinker, discipline, movement, tradition or work from which the text derives? What intellectual, literary, social, cultural or historical influences are reflected in the text? For each of your conclusions, try to point to specific evidence in the text (e.g. terms, ideas, arguments, writing style, etc.) which supports your conclusion. Be careful that your conclusions do not exceed the evidence upon which they rest.

TEXT ONE

God is now throwing Christianity away and is now establishing a new religion . . . All the Christians in the world are destined to be absorbed by our movement. There have been saints, prophets, many religious leaders . . . in past human history . . . Master here is more than any of these people and greater than Jesus himself.[1]

TEXT TWO

Listening to the Lord's glory, singing of Him, thinking of Him, serving His feet, performing His worship, saluting Him, serving Him, friendship with Him, declaring oneself as His [surrendering oneself to Him] - if man could offer unto the Lord devotion of these nine kinds, that indeed I would consider as the greatest lesson one has learned. . . One should engage himself in singing of Me, praising Me, dancing with My themes, imitating My exploits and acts, narrating My stories or listening to them.[2]

PART FIVE   SELF-TEST

A) Definitions and Descriptions - Write your own definition or description of each of the following terms, individuals or texts. After completing the self-test, check your answer with the definition or description given in the textbook.

1. ISKCON _____

_____

_____ .

2. Solar Deity _____
_____
_____.

3. Twelvers _____
_____
_____.

4. esoteric _____
_____
_____.

5. Moroni _____
_____
_____.

6. Bab _____
_____
_____.

B) Multiple Choice

1. The leader of the Baha'i movement who was known as the Bab was

   a. Baha'u'llah
   b. Effendi Rabbani
   c. Sayyid Ali Muhammad
   d. Caitanya

2. The founder of the Mormon movement who was shown the Book of Mormon by the angel Moroni was

   a. Joseph Smith
   b. Brigham Young
   c. Henry Olcott
   d. H. P. Blavatsky

3. The Unification Church believes a new Messiah must come because who did not properly prepare the way?

   a. Jesus Christ
   b. Confucius
   c. Buddha
   d. John the Baptist

4. In the Unification Church there is a strong emphasis on values from what religious tradition?

   a. Confucianism
   b. Buddhism
   c. Shinto
   d. Bon

5. Theosophy was started by who?

   a. Annie Bessant
   b. Krishnamurti
   c. H.P. Blavatsky
   d. Reverand Sun Myung Moon

C) True-False

T   F   1. One of the most unique things about Mormons today is their practice of polygamy.

T   F   2. The main governing body of the Baha'i faith today is the Universal Court of Justice.

T   F   3. The movement known as ISKCON has its roots in the Bhahkti movement of Caitanya.

T   F   4. One of the chief aims of the Baha'i faith is attaining world peace.

T   F   5. Krishnamurti began under the guidance of the Theosophy movement, but left at a later date.

PART SIX   ESSAY AND DISCUSSION QUESTIONS

1. Examine the influences on Theosophy, and how Theosophy made use of those influences. Do you think the author is right when he suggests that Theosophy is a movement whose time has passed?

2. Describe how ISKCON differs, if at all, from orthodox Hinduism? Why is this not just another sect within the larger Hindu movement?

3. Examine in what sense Mormonism can be seen as a truly
   American religious movement? Is it more American than the
   other movements detailed in this chapter?

PART SEVEN   CONFRONTING QUESTIONS AND ISSUES

   Some scholars have tried to draw a distinction between
"religions" and "cults". They have argued that "cults" use
coercion to attract new members, and take away the
individuality of the person. Each person in a cult gives up
his self in order to sink into the group consciousness.
Religions, these scholars argue, do not use such brainwashing
practices and do not gain new members by false advertising.
Other scholars have failed to see a distinction here. They
point out that many religions that are respectable today
began as ecstatic movements.

   Consider this issue, using the religions discussed in this
chapter as a test case. What do these religions do or
believe that the more established religions do not believe or
undertake? Have these religions begun to moderate their
beliefs and practices? Does this suggest that they might be
moving from "cult" status to "religion" status? Have some of
these religions become more mainstream than others? Is this
distinction really valid?

PART EIGHT   AN ESSAY FOR DEEPER CONSIDERATION

Essay Question

   Write an essay question on a topic to do with the more
recent world religions that you have studied in this chapter.
The essay question should poses a problem which interests you
and the answer to which would allow us to better understand
these recent world religions.

   When you are satisfied with your essay question, write an
essay addressing that question.

Tips for Answering

Any good essay addresses a real problem. What is meant by a " problem?" In the context of an academic inquiry, the word "problem" has at least two aspects. First, it refers to a significant issue or question for intellectual inquiry. For example, the question whether fifty-five or fifty-six soldiers were killed at a certain battle is probably not a significant issue. The question of whether this battle was the turning point in the war, however, might very well be a significant issue. Second, a "problem" usually implies an issue for which there is no clear-cut answer. The question of what time it is can be resolved with a high degree of accuracy. Questions such as which battle was the turning point, or what is the meaning of the play The Bacchae allow for a variety of good answers. Such problems require you to examine the evidence and decide which answer makes the best sense.

The problem that you select should be one that interests you. An issue that you are not interested in will, most likely, not interest your readers. It should be one that you believe makes a difference in the way it is answered. For most people the type of questions raised by the world religions are such problems.

There is an infinite variety of such issues that the more recent religions call to mind. For example, many of these movements use fund-raising and recruitment techniques that some people find objectionable. How does a religion get started; what elements need to be present when a religion is a success. Another possible area is the relation between the new religions and the religion to which they are indebted. Yet another area is that of the relation of such religions and government regulation or opposition. Finally, you could examine the question of cult and religions. Are they the same or are they different?

Try to keep the topic you select small and manageable. Remember that this will be a short essay, so you should not tackle an issue that would require a book to be adequately examined. One suggestion is to try to put into your question some limiting clauses. For example, rather than write on "Polygamy in Mormonism", you could focus on "The Problem of Joseph Smith's Views on Polygamy as contained in a selection of his letters." If you find it helpful, you can use the following template to structure your topic: "The Problem of [insert topic] in the [insert work or writing] of [insert name of person or organization] " This gives you a structure of the essay without dictating your content. It also helps you to include some qualifiers in the topic.

PART NINE   PROJECTS FOR DEVELOPING RELIGIOUS EMPATHY

1. The religions that you have studied in this chapter are recent world religions. New religions are being born constantly. Many of these new faiths will never gain many adherents and will die almost unnoticed. A few will, however, gain enough members to survive or move beyond their narrow geographical area. Of these, a small handful may go on to become truly "world religions".

   Many newsstands sell magazines that might be called "New Age" journals. These magazines focus on an array of different movements, gurus, techniques and spiritual retreats. See if you can find such a magazine at the newsstand or at your library. Skim the entire magazine, noticing the type of articles that it contains. Read in more depth a few of the articles that interest you or seem the most unusual. After you are through studying the magazine, consider some questions: What type of movements does the magazine seem aimed at? Are the movements or teachers from established religious traditions or are they from new traditions? If they are from new traditions, can you tell if they are ones that have been influenced by older traditions? Do certain types of religion seem more common than other types? Are certain types of religion or certain strands of religion missing altogether? Why might this be?

2. For many people the type of religious behavior exhibited by the followers of religions such as the Unification Church or ISKCON is immoral or unethical. They do not think they are religions at all; instead they are labeled as "cults". But is this distinction really valid? Do not all religions go through an early stage when their followers act outrageously?

To get a perspective on this issue, and to see that it is
not a problem only for modern man, read the famous play by
Euripides, The Bacchae. This is a play about many things,
but it is certainly a play about new religious movements
and how they are welcomed or condemned. When you read it,
consider the reaction of the King, Pentheus. What is his
view of the new god, Dionysus? Does he think the behavior
of the women who follow the god is respectable? What
happens as the result of his actions? What might such a
play show us about how religions are formed and why people
are drawn to new religious movements.

ANSWER KEY TO SELF-TEST

B) Multiple Choice

1. c
2. b
3. d
4. a
5. c

C) True-False

1. F
2. F
3. T
4. T
5. T

Notes

[1]"The Secret Sayings of 'Master' Moon", <u>Time Magazine</u>, Vol. 107, No.25 (June 14, 1976) 39.

[2]<u>Bhagavata Purana</u>, 7.5.24, 11.27.7, <u>Sources of Indian Tradition</u>, ed. William de Bary, et al., Vol I (New York: Columbia University Press, 1958) 333, 336.

Chapter 11

LIVING WITH RELIGIOUS PLURALISM

PART ONE   LEARNING OBJECTIVES

Doing these exercises, in conjunction with reading the
textbook, should help you to achieve the following
objectives. Read them and see how many you already have
mastered; then study the following terms and concepts, and
work through the exercises. After you have completed all
the exercises, return to this section and review the
objectives again.

You should be able to:

1. Define the concept of "civil religion", illustrate how
   civil religion functions in our society and discuss the
   historical development of civil religion in America.

2. Define the concept of "religious pluralism", illustrate

how religious pluralism functions in our society and discuss the historical development of religious pluralism in America. You should also be able to cite and discuss the views of three scholars on "religious pluralism."

3. Give a brief sketch of the place of Judaism in American history and in America today.

4. Give a brief sketch of the place of Roman Catholicism in American history and in America today.

5. Name at least five Protestant groups with origins in the Reformation, and give a brief indication of their role in American pluralism.

6. Name at least three other Protestant groups that have had an important role to play in American religious pluralism, and indicate the basic nature of these groups.

7. Indicate the basic role that the Eastern Orthodox Church has played in America.

8. Name at least three forms of Buddhism that have taken hold in America, and discuss the problems that might be inhibiting greater integration of Buddhism in American life.

9. Discuss at least three different areas in which Islam has taken hold in American life, and give a brief sketch of the place of Islam in American history and in America today.

10. Compare and contrast the Worldviews of Asian religions and Western religions.

11. Suggest ways in which you can help make the religious pluralism and civil religion that surrounds us enter into your life.

PART TWO   TERMS AND INDIVIDUALS

A) Terms and Concepts

religious pluralism   civil religion

Jehovah's Witness

Puritans

Deism

Church of England (Anglican)

First Amendment

Marranos

Ashkenazim

Sephardim

Anti-Defamation League

Roman Catholics

American Protestant Assoc.

Know-Nothing Party

Ku Klux Klan

Second Vatican Council

Episcopal church

Separatists

Baptists

Quakers

Presbyterians

Methodists

Lutherans

the black church

Eastern Orthodox Church

The Church of Christ, Scientist

Buddhism

World Parliament of Religions

Rinzai Zen Buddhism

Jôdô Shinshû

Pure Land Buddhism

Nichiren Shôshû Sokagakkai

Buddhist Virha Society

Tibetan Nyingma Meditation Cn.

Karme-Choling

Federation of Islamic Assoc.

Muslim Student Assoc.

Nation of Islam

Sunni Islam

American Muslim Association

sage

prophet

anatta

materialism

spiritualism

theism

noumenon

phenomenon

B) Individuals

Jean-Jacques Rousseau

John Locke

Thomas Jefferson

George Washington

Benjamin Franklin

Robert N. Bellah

John F. Kennedy

George Calvert

Martin Luther

Anne Hutchinson

Roger Williams

William Penn

John Calvin

John Knox

John Witherspoon

John Wesley

Ralph Abernathy

Jesse Jackson

Martin Luther King, Jr.

Andrew Young

Billy Graham

Oral Roberts

M. G. "Pat" Robertson

Mary Baker Eddy

Martin E. Marty

Will Herberg

Soryu Kagahi

Soyen Shaku

Soyen Shaku

Daisaku Ikeda

Timothy Drew

W. D. Fard

Elijah (Poole) Muhammad

Malcolm X

Wallace Dean Muhammad

Louis Farrakhan

Ralph Waldo Emerson

Henry David Thoreau

Swami Vivekananda   Sri Ramakrishna
Isaiah   Paul Tillich
Wilfred Cantwell Smith   John Hick
Immanuel Kant

C) Texts

The Constitution of the United States of America
The Bill of Rights   (First Amendment)
Science and Health with Key to the Scriptures
Protestant-Catholic-Jew

PART THREE   GUIDED REVIEW

1. This chapter focuses on two concepts that scholars have used to try to understand the phenomenon of American religion: _____ and _____.

2. Two examples of events in American life that might be examples of the functioning of Civil Religion are _____ and _____.

3. The French philosopher who might have coined the term "civil religion" was _____.

4. Many of the Founding Fathers shared a belief, termed _____ that God created a law-abiding world.

5. The modern sociologist who is associated with the concept of "American civil religion" is _____. He might give the following description of American civil religion: _____
_____.

6. Examples in America of civil religious holidays might be _____ or _____.

7. "Religious pluralism" can be defined as _____
_____.

8. The first Jews came to America with _____.
The three major waves of Jewish immigrations were those of
_____, _____ and
_____.

9. The Jewish group that has done much to teach Americans
about the dangers of discrimination and prejudice is the
_____.

10. A new era of acceptance for American Roman Catholics may
have begun with _____.

11. Groups in American history that attempted to promote
anti-Catholic teachings were _____
and _____.

12. The settlers in Jamestown, Virginian belong to the
_____ church.

13. The Puritans believed that the Church of England should
have more purification from the influences of _____
_____.

14. The Baptists derived their name because they practiced
_____.

15. The Quakers who settled in Pennsylvania differed from
the Puritans in their view of other religions in that they
_____.

16. The Methodist church spread their message in America by
using a "method" that included _____
_____.

17. Although blacks participated in established Protestant
denominations, many blacks developed _____
_____.

18. Protestant preachers who operated outside strict
denominational control and formed their own crusades can be
termed _____.

19. The founder of the Church of Christ, Scientist, was
_____.

20. The famous book in which Will Herberg argued that
Americans retain much of their cultural identity in the
American melting pot through their religious faiths, which
are all seen as acceptable American faiths, is termed
_____.

21. Charles Prebish argues that Buddhist groups in America,
in order to be viewed as more of an American religion,
should _____.

22. The three major concentrations of Muslims in America are
_____, _____ and
_____.

23. Following Elijah Muhammad, _____
espoused a more traditional form of Islam, while _____
_____ took a view that was more hostile
to whites.

24. The special individuals who reveal the religious
solutions in both Asian and Western religions are more
likely to be _____ in the Asian traditions and
_____ in the Western traditions.

25. The author claims that while non-religious worldviews
may see _____ as the determiners of
ultimate values, in the view of world religions man's role
is to _____ these values.

26. Paul Tillich used the phrase "God above the God of
theism", by which he meant _____
_____.

27. Wilfred Cantwell Smith attributes what appears to be
conflicting truth-claims among world religions to _____
_____.

28. In addressing the problem of conflicting truth-claims
among religions, John Hick used the insights of
_____. This philosopher
differentiated between the _____ and the
_____.

29. Hick addresses the issue of religious pluralism and
conflicting truth-claims by arguing that _____
_____.

30. The author of the textbook suggests continuing to
explore world religions by looking, for example, at
_____ or _____.

PART FOUR   ANALYZING TEXTS

   Below are three texts that were not in the textbook.
The texts, however, do contain ideas and concepts with
which you should be familiar after reading the textbook.
Read each text carefully, and try to analyze each by
answering the following questions: What are the main
ideas in the text?   What viewpoint or viewpoints might
the author of the text represent? Is it possible to
identify the specific thinker, discipline, movement,
tradition or work from which the text derives? What
intellectual, literary, social, cultural or historical
influences are reflected in the text? For each of your
conclusions, try to point to specific evidence in the
text (e.g. terms, ideas, arguments, writing style, etc.)
which supports your conclusion. Be careful that your
conclusions do not exceed the evidence upon which they
rest.

TEXT ONE

   In general, then, when a Hindu and a Christian, let us
say, make different statements, neither of them, nor a
Western secularist listening in, is in a position
hastily to determine whether they agree or disagree.
Each statement is made within a total world view; the
meaning of each term of each, as well as of each whole,
derives from the total complex of which it is a more or
less coherent part; the function of religious
statements within each system is itself particular. The
totality within which it obtains not only confers the
meaning upon each term within the statement, and upon
the statement as a whole, but determines also 'the
meaning of meaning' for such statements. . . Yet [a
religious] statement was not put forth as a 'claim' and
to dub it so is insensitive at best. . . The term is
altogether too pretentious. I much prefer, for example,
the standard Islamic notion, of bearing witness. . .
Muslims do not 'claim' that there is no god but God, nor

that Muhammad is His prophet. Rather, they 'bear witness to' these truths (to there 'truths').[1]

TEXT TWO

While some have argued that Christianity is the national faith, and others that church and synagogue celebrate only the generalized religion of "the American Way of Life," few have realized that there actually exists alongside of and rather clearly differentiated from the churches an elaborate and well-institutionalized civil religion in America. . . Considering the separation of church and state, how is a president justified in using the word God at all? The answer is that the separation of church and state has not denied the political realm a religious dimension. Although matters of personal religious belief, worship, and association are considered to be strictly private affairs, there are, at the same time, certain common elements of religious orientation that the great majority of Americans share. These have played a crucial role in the development of American institutions and still provide a religious dimension for the whole fabric of American life, including the political sphere. This public religious dimension is expressed in a set of beliefs, symbols and rituals that I am calling American civil religion. [2]

TEXT THREE

Two doctrines are opposed if they cannot be accepted jointly without absurdity. To accept a doctrine which recommends a course of action is to undertake to do what is recommended. So two doctrines are opposed if no one could undertake both courses of action without absurdity. . . So two assertions are in opposition if it would be absurd to take both what is said in one and what is said in the other as true. Thus doctrines which assert something are opposed if they are contrary to one another or if they are contradictory to one another. . . In general, what is being said in the utterance of some doctrine depends on the rules by which its concepts operate, and often we find what these are by trying out objections. So one way we could learn the rules of relevance and consistency of some scheme of religious doctrines would be to see what opposition it countenances and hence what objections its proponents can admit.[3]

PART FIVE   SELF-TEST

A) Definitions and Descriptions - Write your own definition or description of each of the following terms, individuals or texts. After completing the self-test, check your answer with the definition or description given in the textbook.

1. Baptists _____

_____

_____.

2. phenomenon _____

_____

_____.

3. John Wesley _____

_____

_____.

4. religious pluralism _____

_____

_____.

5. Malcolm X _____

_____

_____.

6. civil religion _____

_____

_____.

7. First Amendment _____

_____

_____.

8. sage _____

_____

_____.

9. Know-Nothing Party _____
_____
_____.

10. Nation of Islam _____
_____
_____.

B) Multiple Choice

1. The theologian who used the phrase "God above the God of theism" was

   a. Wilfred Cantwell Smith
   b. John Hick
   c. Paul Tillich
   d. Rudolph Otto

2. Which of the following was not an influence on the Founding Fathers' religion and civil institutions?

   a. Deism
   b. Islam
   c. John Locke
   d. Freemasons

3. Which of the following formed the Nation of Islam?

   a. Malcolm X
   b. W. D. Fard
   c. Elijah Muhammad
   d. Noble Drew Ali

4. The term "civil religion" was first coined by

   a. Robert N. Bellah
   b. John Hick
   c. James A Christenson
   d. Jean-Jacques Rousseau

5. The philosopher from whom Hick derived his notion of "phenomenon/noumenon" was

   a. Immanuel Kant
   b. David Hume

    c. Soren Kierkegaard
    d. himself

6. The group that William Penn belonged to and that preached religious tolerance was the

    a. Quakers
    b. Puritans
    c. Separatists
    d. Shakers

7. Which is <u>not</u> among the waves of Jewish immigrants mentioned in the book?

    a. Sephardic
    b. Ashkenazim
    c. Ethiopian
    d. Eastern European

8. What is known as the Church of England in England is known as what in the United States?

    a. Congregational
    b. Episcopal
    c. Methodist
    d. Baptist

9. What Catholic was given a charter by King Charles I to found a colony in America?

    a. Roger Williams
    b. William Penn
    c. John Newman
    d. George Calvert

10. The Protestant group that spread its message by using revival meetings and circuit riders was

    a. Baptists.
    b. Episcopal church.
    c. Methodist church.
    d. Lutheran church.

C) True-False

T F   1. The Buddhist Church of America is an
             American form of Nichiren Buddhism.

T F   2. Because of the separation of Church and
             State in America, prayers are not allowed
             to be said in schools or at government
             functions.

T F   3. Congress is forbidden from establishing any
             religion by the Constitution.

T F   4. The first Jews to come to America were
             those who came to New York city in 1692.

T F   5. Baptists were so named because they
             practiced and believed in adult immersion
             baptism.

T F   6. George Washington was the author of
             Virginia's Statute of Religious Freedom.

T F   7. The American Protestant Association was
             organized in order to promote harmony
             between Protestants and Catholics.

T F   8. W. C. Smith argued that each religion
             should be judged by its own standards of
             truth.

T F   9. Religious pluralism is defined as living
             among many religions all claiming to be
             true.

T F   10.The Black church has played a major role in
             advancing the aspirations of Black people.

PART SIX   ESSAY AND DISCUSSION QUESTIONS

1. Analyze Robert Bellah's theory concerning American civil
   religion. What appears to be Bellah's definition of
   "American civil religion?" Is there such a dimension to
   American religious life?

2. Explain the structure of American religious pluralism as it exists today.

3. Charles Prebish argues that Buddhist groups have to make a more public witness before Americans will view Buddhism as an American religion. Do you think he is correct? What do you think "a more public witness" means? Are some religious groups or movements, perhaps Buddhism, just to non-American to ever be fully at home here?

4. What do you think are the fundamental differences and similarities between religions of Asia and religions of the West? Back up your analysis with illustrations from these traditions.

5. Analyze two examples of religious intolerance in American history. What can be learned through these examples of intolerance?

6. Explain John Hick's theory of religious pluralism. Is it even meaningful to talk of a noumenal God, since all such talk must be structured by our "mental additives?"

PART SEVEN   CONFRONTING QUESTIONS AND ISSUES

The First Amendment of the Constitution of the United States of America can be seen as containing two different enjoinders on religious liberty. The First Amendment states: "Congress shall make no law respecting an establishment of religion or prohibiting the free exercise thereof." Many Constitutional scholars have maintained that there is a tension in this passage between the stipulation that nothing be done to prohibit the peoples right to practice their religion, and the prohibition on government establishing religious practices. Since the Constitution is not self-interpreting, the Supreme Court over the years has been required to interpret this clause in order to reach decisions on cases that have come before it. It has turned to three main ideas or standards in order to interpret this passage.

One idea or metaphor the Court has used is that of a "wall of separation". According to this idea, the First Amendment is read as requiring a more or less complete separation between religious practices and governmental functions. Religious symbols or ceremonies on (Federal) government property would probably be deemed unconstitutional under this standard. The second metaphor the Court has used is that of "strict neutrality." This standard is not as stringent as the idea of a "wall of separation." It does not mandate a complete separation between government and religion, but only that government be neutral in its dealings with different religious organizations. Government should neither favor religion, nor hinder religion. More recently, a third idea emerged during the Burger court, that of "excessive entanglement." This metaphor would appear to allow the greatest cooperation between government and religion; governments might be able to provide certain aid or benefits to religious groups as long as they did not do so "excessively." The issue of what precisely constitutes "excessive entanglement", however, would need clarification, and it is not at all clear whether an objective definition is possible.

In recent years many politicians and citizens have lobbied in favor of "tuition tax-credits" for parents who send their children to non-public schools. This plan would grant a tax write-off or deduction to parents who pay private school tuition. While many non-religious groups are in support of this plan, religious organizations who operate religiously affiliated schools would clearly benefit from such legislation. The possibility of a tax-break would serve to attract students and allow the schools to increase their fees. But would such a law violate the First Amendment of the Constitution?

Imagine that you are a Supreme Court justice who has to rule on the constitutionality of tuition tax-credits. How would you interpret the First Amendment? What influence would the history in this country of "civil religion" and "religious pluralism" have on your decision? What are the dangers and benefits of each of the three standards? Would you use one of the three to help decide this case? If so, which standard do you think is most useful, and why? What would be your ruling?

PART EIGHT   AN ESSAY FOR DEEPER CONSIDERATION

Essay Question

It is popularly believed that religious pluralism and non-competition between religions go hand-in-hand. An argument could be made, however, that the primary advantage of religious pluralism is that it increases the possibility for competition between religions. Study the following argument, which reflects ideas put forth in the writings of William Christian and Anthony Flew.

Religious texts and believers make statements concerning the world, the Absolute and the relation of human beings to both. To make a statement is to say that such and such is the case. And, it follows, that to say such and such is the case necessarily implies that some other state of affairs is not the case. Therefore, if religious believers are making significant claims about reality, they must also be denying other, competing claims about reality. It follows from this that opposition between religious doctrines is a sign that something significant is being stated and debated.

When political parties agree on most issues and cooperate it is usually a sign that neither party is making any significant statement about the world, and its recommendations for action. Disagreements between Democrats and Republicans, between Communists and Capitalists indicate that something decisive is at issue. Competition and the battle for control of the public mind only occurs when the alternatives are well thought-out and propose course of action that matter. If this is the case, then it follows that the different religious groups in this country should be competing with their full energy for adherents and influence. If there is no real opposition between religious groups and their doctrines, then religions must not be saying anything significant. And if religions are uttering significant truth-claims whose acceptance makes a real difference in our lives, then religions should want all people to accept these truths, and should use all ethical means at their disposal to win converts and demolish opposing claims. Fierce competition between religious groups is a sign that religion really counts for something.

Analyze and evaluate the above argument in an essay.

Tips for Answering

This essay assignment is asking you to analyze and critique an argument. Here are three suggestions on how to prepare to write your essay.

First, the essay question states that this argument was influenced by the ideas of two philosophers of religion, William Christian and Anthony Flew. In order to more fully understand the argument you might want to read the writings of one or both of these philosophers.[4] The writing by Flew has been very influential in the study of religion, and is quite short. The book by Christian is much longer, but contains ideas that you might want to use in your essay.

Second, you will need to evaluate the soundness of the argument. In order to do this you might want to consider the following questions: Are there different parts to the argument, or smaller arguments within the major argument? If so, it might be helpful to outline the reasons and conclusion in each part of the argument. What reasons are given for each conclusion, and are they strong enough to warrant the conclusion? Does the argument over-generalize? Does it paint certain questions as black-and-white, and ignore a middle position? What assumptions does the argument make, and are these assumptions valid?

Third, while the argument does not refer to historical facts, it does seem to imply some historical basis and consequences. For example, it implies that competition among religious groups and their ideas results in healthier religious groups. From your study of religion in the United States, do you believe this is the case? What relevancy might historical evidence have for the soundness of this argument?

PART NINE   PROJECTS FOR DEVELOPING RELIGIOUS EMPATHY

1. The author of the textbook makes the argument that the experience of religion in America is marked by religious pluralism. Frequently, one of the best places to observe this pluralism in action is the university campus. There are a number of reasons that campuses offer a wide mix of

religious groups. College students often feel a
dissatisfaction with the religion that they were brought
up with and want to explore other options. There is some
evidence that young adulthood is a time when we are more
likely to feel the need to ask spiritual or profound
questions. And perhaps for this reason, many religious
groups find the college environment a fruitful hunting
ground for new adherents. Whatever the reasons, your
campus may be the perfect environment for the study of
religious pluralism.

Consider what location on your campus gives you the best
opportunity to observe many student religious groups.
Many colleges have a main walk or quad along which student
organizations set up their tables. At other schools the
student union or student center has space set aside for
this purpose. A student organization day may offer the
best chance to observe religious pluralism.

If you visit such a location, try taking some time to
observe each group. How does each group try to gain the
students attention and attract their interest? If you
have taken a course in marketing or public relations, try
to apply what you learned in that course to "the selling
of religion." If a group is using banners or slogans,
what is its "sales approach?" Do different groups take
different approaches, and if so, why do you think that is?
How do the people at each table interact with the students
who stop at the table? After observing from a distance,
you might want to visit each table. Is the approach of
the person at the table low-key or high pressure? Does
the group appear to be merely interested in disseminating
information, or does it appear to be seeking new members?
Is the group interested in political action? Does the
group seem to be interested in the entire student
population, or only certain sub-groups (Catholics, Jews,
Blacks, etc.). Which approaches would you judge to be the
most effective? What conclusions can you draw concerning
how religious pluralism functions in our country?

2. Robert Bellah's theory of a "civil religion" has been a
   very influential one, but also a controversial one. Not
   all scholars agree with the view that there is such a
   separate religious tradition in our country. You might
   want to test out Bellah's theory for yourself.

The textbook gives you a very good indication of where to start looking for the American Civil Religion. You will probably be able to think of other dimensions, but here are a couple of suggestions. One type of event that Bellah mentions is major Presidential addresses. This would include, of course, Inauguration speeches, State of the Union addresses and any major televised speech. Consider the following questions as you watch such an address. What references are made, if any, to God, and to the notion of America as doing God's work? Are the references to God ones that almost any Catholic, Protestant, Jew or Muslim would find acceptable? Are there any references in the speech that you would consider as advancing the position of a particular religious group? Do the references to God appear to be only a ceremonial "tip of the hat?" Does the President use any other religious metaphors or symbols?

Another place to look for American Civil Religion is at the "non-religious" National Holidays. An obvious candidate would be Thanksgiving, a holiday with religious over-tones, but not one directly linked to the Christian liturgical calender. Less obvious examples might be Martin Luther King Day and Mother's Day. In each case, consider the "rituals" that are performed on the holiday: What civic functions do the rituals perform? How do they help to define us as Americans? Are there religious elements to these actions, and if so, what are they? Again, is the religious element a general one, or one linked to a specific religious tradition? What do these holidays tell us about American Civil Religion?

ANSWER KEY TO SELF-TEST

B) Multiple Choice

1. c	6. a
2. b	7. c
3. c	8. b
4. d	9. d
5. a	10. c

C) <u>True-False</u>

1.	F	6.	F
2.	F	7.	F
3.	T	8.	T
4.	F	9.	T
5.	T	10.	T

Notes

[1]Wilfred Cantwell Smith, "Conflicting Truth-Claims: A Rejoinder," Truth and Dialogue in World Religions: Conflicting Truth-Claims, ed. John Hick, (Philadelphia: The Westminster Press, 1974) 158.

[2]Robert N. Bellah, "Civil Religion in America", Daedalus, Vol. 96, No. 1 (Winter 1967).

[3]William Christian, Oppositions of Religious Doctrines (New York: Herder and Herder, 1972) 2, 13.

[4]Anthony Flew, et. al., "Theology and Falsification," New Essays in Philosophical Theology, ed. Anthony Flew and Alasdair MacIntyre (London: SCM Press, 1955) 96-108.

William Christian, Oppositions of Religious Doctrines (New York: Herder and Herder, 1972).

Appendix

MARXISM AND WORLD RELIGIONS

PART ONE   LEARNING OBJECTIVES

Doing these exercises, in conjunction with reading the
textbook, should help you to achieve the following
objectives. Read them and see how many you already have
mastered; then study the following terms and concepts, and
work through the exercises. After you have completed all the
exercises, return to this section and review the objectives
again.

You should be able to:

1. Write a brief outline of the life of Karl Marx, and
   indicate his role in the development of communism.

2. Name and discuss at least two major thinkers who
   influenced the thought of Karl Marx.

3. Explain Marx's position on class struggle, his understanding of the dialectic, and his view of the role religion plays in society and history.

4. Write a brief outline of the life of Lenin, and indicate his role in guiding Russia towards communism.

5. Analyze how religions were viewed and treated in the Soviet Union by the government, the Party and the people from the time of the Russian Revolution until the end of the Cold War.

6. Write a brief outline of the life of Mao, and indicate his role in establishing communism in China and governing China from 1949 to 1976.

7. Understand what were some of Mao's contacts with and views of the teachings and philosophy of traditional China.

8. Analyze how religions and traditional teachings were viewed and treated in China by the government, the Party and the people from the time of the Chinese Revolution until the summer of 1989.

9. Discuss and write about the Marxist Worldview; in particular, the Marxist view of the world and the role of humans in the world, the fundamental problem and resolution for human beings, life after death, and the nature of organized religion.

10. Address and debate the problem of whether Marxism should be seen as a "religion" or whether it is the rejection of all religions.

PART TWO   TERMS AND INDIVIDUALS

A) Terms and Concepts

Marxism
thesis
synthesis
Tienanman Square
Manchu (Ch'ing) Dynasty
humanism

the dialectic
antithesis
capitalism
League of the Militant Godless
Cultural Revolution

B) Individuals

Karl Marx	Georg Wilhelm Friedrich Hegel
Friedrich Engles	Ludwig Feuerbach
Vladimir Ilyich Lenin	Mao Tse-tung
Joseph Stalin	Mikhail Gorbachev
Deng Xiaoping	

C) Texts

Capital: A Critique of Political Economy
The Communist Manifesto
The Essence of Christianity
The Development of Capitalism in Russia
Imperialism, The Highest Stage of Capitalism
The State and Revolution

D) Individuals and Terms From Other Traditions

Chiang K'ai-shek	Henry Kissinger
President Richard Nixon	Pope John Paul II ,
Protestant Christianity	Judaism
Russian Orthodox Church	Ukrainian Catholic Church

PART THREE   GUIDED REVIEW

1. Until recently, in most communist countries the practice
of religion was _____. However, today in
many of these countries the practice of religion is
_____.

2. Marxism is based on the thought of _____.

3. The author of the textbook claims that religion, for Marx,
was a _____, and not a _____.

4. Marx took the method of dialectical reasoning from the
writings of _____.

5. _____ supported Marx and his family,
and collaborated with Marx on many writings, including The
Communist Manifesto.

6. Whereas Hegel believed reality was ultimately _____, Marx argued that it was ultimately _____.

7. The theory of the dialectic held that a _____ is confronted by a _____, from which emerges a new _____. This dialectic was used to explain the history of class struggle.

8. The forerunner of Marx who argued that religion was only the projection of man's desires upon the material universe was _____.

9. Marx believed that religion was used by _____ to help oppress _____.

10. Workers who had to endure poverty and the appropriation of the fruits of their labor by the bourgeoisie might be pacified by religion which promised _____ _____.

11. Marx is famous for calling religion the _____ _____.

12. The leader of the Bolshevik party and the chief figure in the success of the Russian Revolution was _____.

13. In theory, the people of the USSR had freedom to practice their religion as long as that religion did not _____ _____.

14. Between the years 1917 and 1940, the attitude of the Soviet state towards religion could be described as _____ _____.

15. Two examples of the changes that have occurred in the last ten years in the official Soviet view of religion are _____ and _____.

16. The main leader of the Chinese Revolution was _____ _____.

17. During the Cultural Revolution in China the party and the government _____ religion.

18. While Mao was a dedicated communist, at times in his life he also studied and was influenced by _____
_____.

19. In June of 1989, the Chinese government reacted to the student and worker protest in Tienanmen Square by _____
_____.

20. Marxism believes that the highest value in the universe is not _____, but is _____.
Therefore, most Marxists would _____ atheism.

21. According to Marxism, individual ability should be used not for private gain but for _____.

22. To the extent a Marxist believes in immortality, it would lie in _____.

23. The argument could be made that Marxism functions as a religion because it _____
_____.

PART FOUR   ANALYZING TEXTS

   Below are three texts that were not in the textbook.
The texts, however, do contain ideas and concepts with
which you should be familiar after reading the textbook.
Read each text carefully, and try to analyze each by
answering the following questions: What are the main
ideas in the text?   What viewpoint or viewpoints might
the author of the text represent? Is it possible to
identify the specific thinker, discipline, movement,
tradition or work from which the text derives? What
intellectual, literary, social, cultural or historical
influences are reflected in the text? For each of your
conclusions, try to point to specific evidence in the
text (e.g. terms, ideas, arguments, writing style, etc.)
which supports your conclusion. Be careful that your
conclusions do not exceed the evidence upon which they
rest.

TEXT ONE

A man in China is usually subjected to the domination of
three systems of authority: 1)the system of the state
(political authority), ranging from the national,
provincial, and county government to the township
government; 2)the system of the clan (clan authority),
ranging from the central and branch ancestral temples to
the head of the household; and 3) the system of gods and
spirits (theocratic authority), including the system of
the nether world ranging from the King of Hell to the
city gods and local deities, and that of supernatural
beings ranging from the Emperor of Heaven to all kinds
of gods and spirits. As to women, apart from being
dominated by the three systems mentioned above, they are
further dominated by men (the authority of the husband).
. . . Theocratic authority begins to totter everywhere
as the peasant movement develops. In many places the
peasant associations have taken over the temples of the
gods as their offices. Everywhere they advocate the
appropriation of temple properties to maintain peasant
schools and to defray association expenses, calling this
"public revenue from superstition." Forbidding
superstition and smashing idols has become quite the
vogue in Liling. . . When a death occurs in a family,
such practices as sacrifice to the gods, performance of
Taoist or Buddhist rites, and offering of sacred lamps
are becoming rare.[1]

TEXT TWO

The history of all hitherto existing society is the
history of class struggles. . . The modern bourgeois
society that has sprouted from the ruins of feudal
society, has not done away with class antagonisms. It
has but established new classes, new conditions of
oppression, new forms of struggle in place of the old
ones. Our epoch, the epoch of the bourgeoisie,
possesses, however, this distinctive feature: It has
simplified the class antagonisms. Society as a whole is
more and more splitting up into two great hostile camps,
into two great classes directly facing each other -
bourgeoisie and proletariat. . . The bourgeoisie has
played a most revolutionary role in history. . . It has
drowned the most heavenly ecstasies of religious fervor,

of chivalrous enthusiasm, of philistine sentimentalism,
in the icy waters of egotistical calculation. It has
resolved personal worth into exchange value, and in
place of the numberless indefeasible chartered freedoms,
has set up that single unconscionable freedom - Free
Trade. In one word, for exploitation, veiled by
religious and political illusions, it has substituted
naked, shameless, direct, brutal exploitation. [2]

PART FIVE   SELF-TEST

A) Definitions and Descriptions - Write your own definition or
description of each of the following terms. After completing
the self-test, check your answer with the definition or
description given in the textbook.

1. antithesis _____
_____
_____ .

2. capitalism _____
_____
_____ .

3. the dialectic _____
_____
_____ .

4. Marxism _____
_____
_____ .

5. League of the Militant Godless _____
_____
_____ .

B) Multiple Choice

1. The friend of Karl Marx who collaborated with him in the
   writing of many of his articles was

   a. Engels
   b. Hegel

    c. Lenin
    d. Feuerbach

2. Lenin led a party in Russia called the

    a. Menshevik party
    b. Christian Democrat party
    c. Bolshevik party
    d. White party

3. An important event for the advancing of religious
tolerance in the Soviet Union was the meeting in 1989
between Mikhail Gorbachev and

    a. the Archbishop of Canterbury
    b. the Dalai Lama
    c. President Carter
    d. Pope John Paul II

4. The most thorough explication of Karl Marx's thought was
his book

    a. The Essence of Christianity
    b. Capital: A Critique of Political Economy
    c. The Protestant Ethic and the Spirit of Capitalism
    d. The Phenomenology of Mind

5. Which of the following is not mentioned as one of the
things Mao did when he came to power?

    a. Nationalized the property of religious institutions.
    b. Denied the privileges of membership in the Community
        party to anyone who practiced religion.
    c. Banned moral teachings from the schools.
    d. Expelled foreign missionaries from China.

C) True-False

T F   1. After 1929 in the Soviet Union, religious
            education could only be given in private
            and to those over the age of eighteen.

T F   2. Marx derived his idea of the dialectic from
            the philosopher David Hume.

T F   3. Although most Marxists do not believe in
                God, they do believe that there is an after-
                life in heaven.

T F   4. Feuerbach believed that there was no super-
                natural realm, only humans projecting their
                desires upon the material universe.

T F   5. Marxism believes that religion is a means
                for the ruling class to oppress the lower
                classes in the economic order.

PART SIX   ESSAY AND DISCUSSION QUESTIONS

1. What do Marxists mean by "the dialectic of history"? Can
   you give any examples from either the Russian or Chinese
   revolutions that might be used by a Marxist to illustrate
   this concept?

2. What do you judge to be the fundamental differences and
   similarities among the three examples of Marxism presented
   in this chapter (those of Marx, Lenin and Mao)?

3. Identify Lenin's role in the Russian Revolution and
   explain his contribution to communism.

4. Explain what rationale a Marxist might give for curtailing
   peoples right to practice or promote religion? How valid
   do you believe this rationale to be? Why?

5. Describe the Marxist worldview, and how such a worldview
   could be distinguished from that of one of the major world
   religions that you have studied?

6. Describe the challenges that Marxism appears to be facing
   today, and predict what future role Marxism will play on
   the world scene.

PART SEVEN   CONFRONTING QUESTIONS AND ISSUES

   It has become fashionable, especially since the collapse
of the Berlin Wall and the emergence of radical change in

Eastern Europe, to talk about the failure of communism and Marxism. Assuredly, Marxist communism has failed to deliver on its economic and social promises in most, if not all, of the countries where it has taken hold. Many of the theories of Marx, of Lenin and of Mao have been shown to be plainly wrong. Nevertheless, there are positions that communists espouse that are not so easily dismissed. For example, it is the communist belief that through history a small number of people have taken economic advantage of the larger mass of humans. They also teach that each person deserves to have their basic human needs met, and that the most fortunate in society must contribute a greater share to the less fortunate. Or, to take one more example, a communist might hold that equality in controlling the means of production is a necessary prerequisite to true human freedom. Whether or not you agree with Marxism or communism, you might agree with some of these positions on the need for social and economic justice.

Based on the knowledge of Marxist communism you gained from reading this chapter, take the position for a moment of a communist. You are not necessarily an orthodox Marxist, but you believe deeply in the fundamental values of economic justice and equality. You also, however, are aware that many of the so-called communist regimes of Eastern Europe were more totalitarian oligarchies, or perversions of communism than true communism. You are grappling with these changes in the world and trying to adapt your faith to them. Given this, what role would you see, if any, for orthodox Marxism in today's world? How could communism be changed so as to retain its best elements and correct its drawbacks, and what would be this best form of communism? What role could this best form of communism play in promoting world justice and equality?

PART EIGHT   AN ESSAY FOR DEEPER CONSIDERATION

Essay Question

The textbook claims that Marxism has functioned, in many ways, as a religion and cites a number of reasons to back up its claim. In an essay examine whether Marxism should or should not be viewed as a religion. Consider both arguments in favor of interpreting Marxism as a religion and arguments for rejecting the view of Marxism as a religion? What is your position on this question, and why?

Tips for Answering

In the Introduction to this study guide you were asked to formulate in an essay a general definition of "religion." Since the time you wrote your essay you have studied a wide array of different religious traditions. It is possible that you have revised your original definition as you have become more knowledgeable about the history of religions. One way to view this essay question is that it is giving you a chance to re-examine and test your definition of "religion" by presenting you with an interesting test case: Marxism.

This essay question asks you to do two things: to examine arguments on both sides of the issue of whether Marxism is a religion, and then to indicate which is the best view, and why. There are a number of ways you could approach this assignment, but here is one suggestion. Whether or not you view Marxism as a religion may hinge on which definition of the term "religion" you use. Marxism may qualify as a religion under certain definitions, and not qualify under other definitions. You could structure your essay, therefore, around an examination of how varying definitions of "religion" would classify Marxism. You also might want to examine what are the strengths and weaknesses of these definitions. This could be the first part of your essay.

In order to determine, however, whether _you_ view Marxism as a religion you will need to develop, present, and defend _your_ definition of "religion." What is your definition and why is this one the most appropriate for studying and classifying religious phenomenon? This would address the second half of the essay question. If you have already formulated a general definition of religion, either at the start of the semester or in the interval since, you could use this definition as your starting point. Consider whether you need to revise your original definition in light of what you have learned this semester. Was your original definition too narrow? Would it fit, for example, both Theravada Buddhism and Confucianism? Was it too broad? If you have not already written down a definition, you will need to come up with a definition of religion that you think will apply to all movements, beliefs or practices that you would consider "religious." You might ask what are the key characteristics

that all the religions you have studied possess? Or, as Rems
Edwards suggests, you might argue that there are no such
shared characteristics but rather a collection of family
traits.

Having presented your definition of religion and why it is
the most useful definition, the final portion of your essay
should study whether Marxism lies within the bounds of your
definition. Does Marxism possess all the key characteristics
of a "religion?" Does it possess some, but not all, of them?
Is it lacking some element that it would need to qualify as a
"religion", and ,if so, which one?

PART NINE   PROJECTS FOR DEVELOPING RELIGIOUS EMPATHY

1. One of the key tenets of Marxism is that society is
   divided into economic classes, and that these classes are
   in competition with each other. While class membership is
   defined economically, the signs of class membership are
   often non-economic. Our language, dress, manner,
   possessions and way of thinking (consciousness) are often
   indications of where we belong in the class structure of
   our society.

   Take a trip with a friend of yours to various parts of the
   city or town where you live. Try and visit sections of
   the town where people from a variety of different classes
   might live or be present. Observe people's manners,
   dress, language or any other relevant behavior. Try to
   note how they act and how they spend their time. What
   about each person is the best indicator of their social
   and economic class? Do you find it difficult in our
   society to gauge someone's position in society, or is it
   obvious from observing them? Do your observations lead
   you to support Marx's view that the classes are in
   competition?

2. Marxism is confronting grave challenges to its future, and
   is struggling to both survive and change. As this text is
   being written the Soviet Union is debating how and how
   rapidly to change its economic system. Simply by reading
   the newspapers everyday you can learn much about Marxism
   its weaknesses, and its viability.

Keep for a month or more a combination scrapbook-journal on Marxism in the contemporary world. Purchase a note book with at least fifty pages. Each day read the newspaper, and cut out any articles or columns that deal with the changes going on in the Soviet Union or Eastern Europe.   Look also for articles on Cuba, and China. Paste each article that seems interesting in your notebook. Then, below each article or on the facing page, write your comments or reflections on the article. How much popular support does Marxism have in various parts of the world?   How are the governments that are communist attempting to deal with events in the world? Does Marxism seem to be changing and adapting, or is it disappearing? Why? At the end of a month review all your notes and reflections. What conclusions can you draw concerning Marxism and its future?

ANSWER KEY TO SELF-TEST SECTION

B) Multiple Choice

1. a
2. c
3. d
4. b
5. c

C) True-False

1. T
2. F
3. F
4. T
5. T

Notes

[1]Mao Tse-tung, "Report on an Investigation of the Hunan Peasant Movement," <u>Sources of Chinese Tradition</u>, ed. William T. de Bary et al., vol. II (New York: Columbia University Press, 1960) 210-211.

[2]Karl Marx and Friedrich Engels, <u>The Communist Manifesto</u> (1888; New York: Appleton-Century-Crofts, 1955) 9-12.